HAL•LEONARD

GUITAR

PLAY-ALONG®

VOL. 53

ISBN 978-1-4234-0056-1

HAL•LEONARD®
CORPORATION

7777 W. BLUEMOUND RD. P.O. BOX 13819 MILWAUKEE, WI 53213

Visit Hal Leonard Online at
www.halleonard.com

VOL. 53

CONTENTS

Guitar Notation Legend

THE MUSICAL STAFF shows pitches and and rhythms and is divided by bar lines into measures. Pitches are named after the first seven letters of the alphabet.

TABLATURE graphically represents the guitar fingerboard. Each horizontal line represents a string, and each number represents a fret.

4th string, 2nd fret   1st & 2nd strings open, played together   open D chord

HALF-STEP BEND: Strike the note and bend up 1/2 step.

WHOLE-STEP BEND: Strike the note and bend up one step.

GRACE NOTE BEND: Strike the note and bend up as indicated. The first note does not take up any time.

SLIGHT (MICROTONE) BEND: Strike the note and bend up 1/4 step.

BEND AND RELEASE: Strike the note and bend up as indicated, then release back to the original note. Only the first note is struck.

PRE-BEND: Bend the note as indicated, then strike it.

VIBRATO: The string is vibrated by rapidly bending and releasing the note with the fretting hand.

PALM MUTING: The note is partially muted by the pick hand lightly touching the string(s) just before the bridge.

HAMMER-ON: Strike the first (lower) note with one finger, then sound the higher note (on the same string) with another finger by fretting it without picking.

PULL-OFF: Place both fingers on the notes to be sounded. Strike the first note and without picking, pull the finger off to sound the second (lower) note.

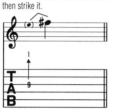

LEGATO SLIDE: Strike the first note and then slide the same fret-hand finger up or down to the second note. The second note is not struck.

SHIFT SLIDE: Same as legato slide, except the second note is struck.

PINCH HARMONIC: The note is fretted normally and a harmonic is produced by adding the edge of the thumb or the tip of the index finger of the pick hand to the normal pick attack.

TRILL: Very rapidly alternate between the notes indicated by continuously hammering on and pulling off.

TAPPING: Hammer ("tap") the fret indicated with the pick-hand index or middle finger and pull off to the note fretted by the fret hand.

NATURAL HARMONIC: Strike the note while the fret-hand lightly touches the string directly over the fret indicated.

TREMOLO PICKING: The note is picked as rapidly and continuously as possible.

VIBRATO BAR DIVE AND RETURN: The pitch of the note or chord is dropped a specified number of steps (in rhythm) then returned to the original pitch.

VIBRATO BAR SCOOP: Depress the bar just before striking the note, then quickly release the bar.

VIBRATO BAR DIP: Strike the note and then immediately drop a specified number of steps, then release back to the original pitch.

Additional Musical Definitions

(accent) • Accentuate note (play it louder)

(staccato) • Play the note short

D.S. al Coda • Go back to the sign (𝄋), then play until the measure marked *"To Coda"*, then skip to the section labelled *"Coda."*

D.S. al Fine • Go back to the beginning of the song and play until the measure marked *"Fine"* (end).

Fill • Label used to identify a brief melodic figure which is to be inserted into the arrangement.

N.C. • Instrument is silent (drops out).

 • Repeat measures between signs.

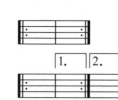 • When a repeated section has different endings, play the first ending only the first time and the second ending only the second time.

Boogie Oogie Oogie

Words and Music by Janice Marie Johnson and Perry Kibble

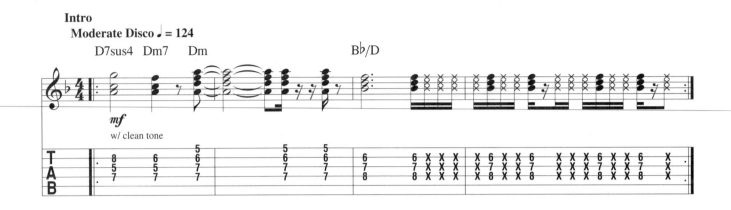

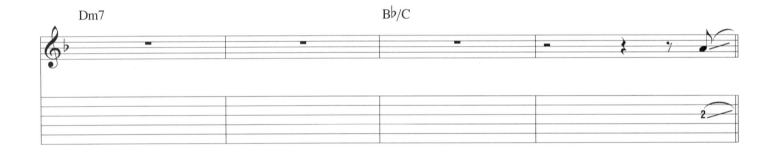

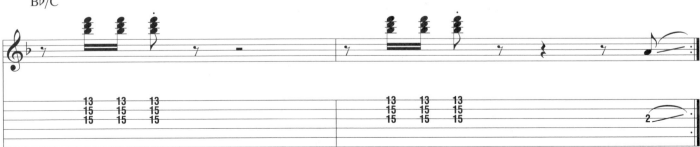

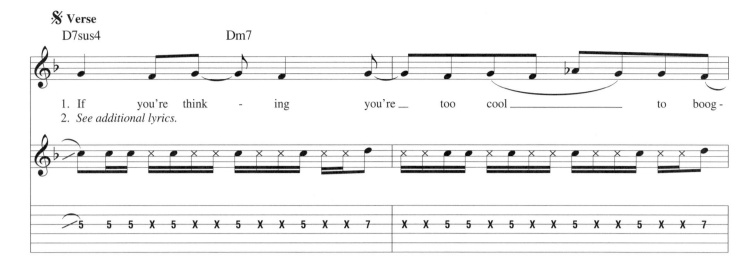

1. If you're think - ing you're ___ too cool ___ to boog -

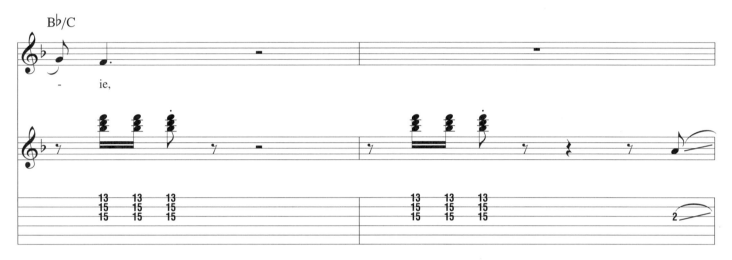

- ie,

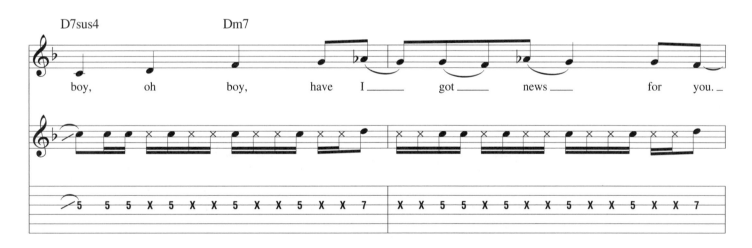

boy, oh boy, have I ___ got ___ news ___ for you. ___

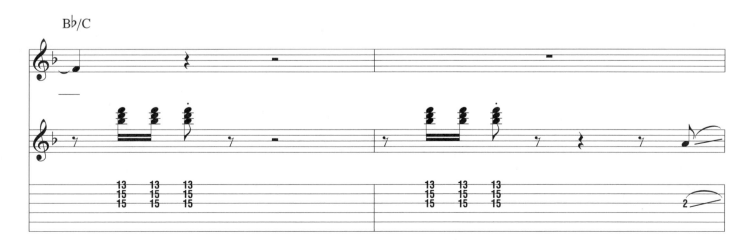

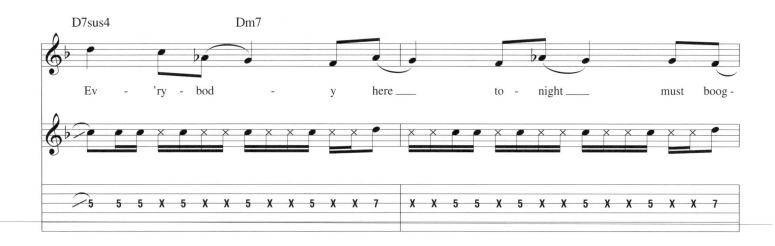

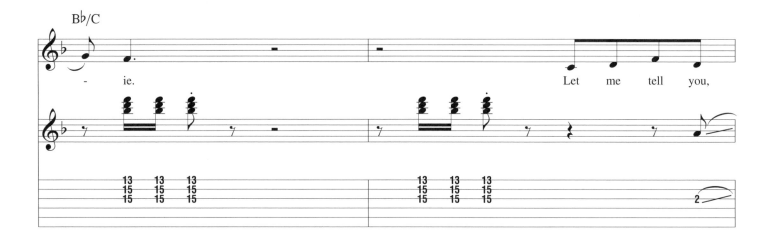

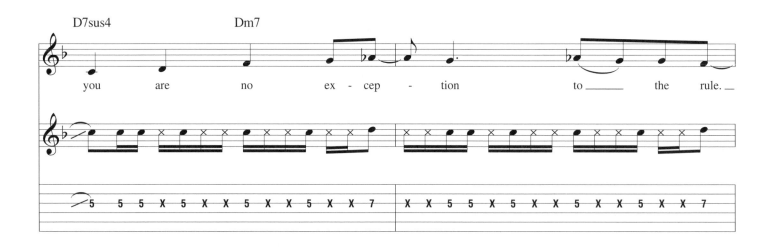

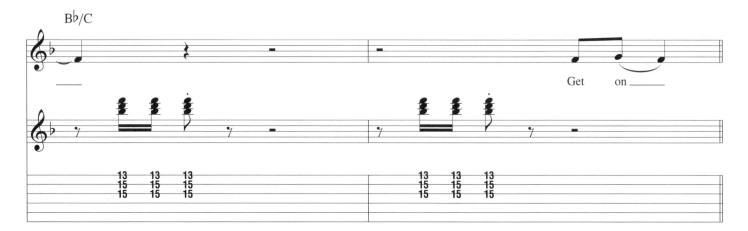

Chorus

up _____ on _____ the floor _____ 'cause _ we're gon - na boog - ie oog - ie oog - ie till we

See additional lyrics

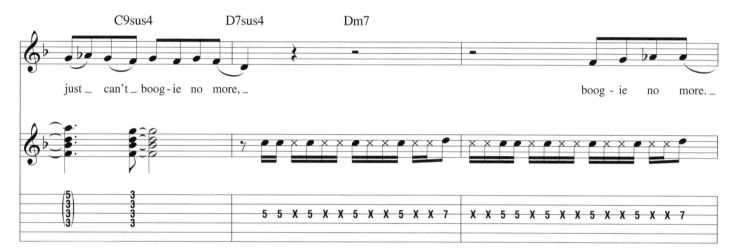

just _ can't _ boog - ie no more, _____ boog - ie no more. _

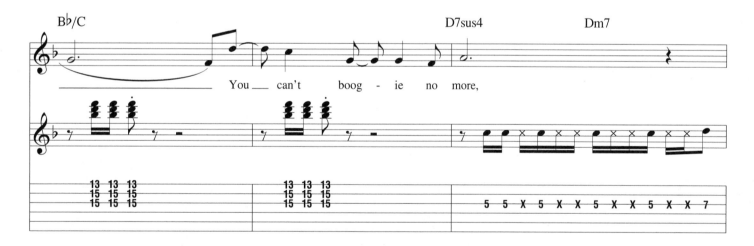

You _____ can't _ boog - ie no more,

To Coda

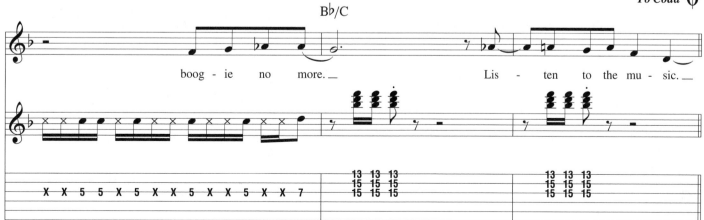

boog - ie no more. _____ Lis - ten to the mu - sic. _

9

Guitar Solo

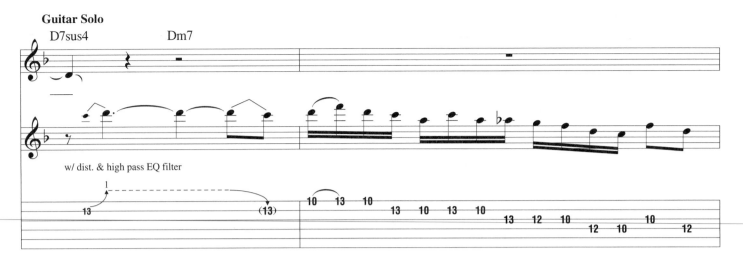

w/ dist. & high pass EQ filter

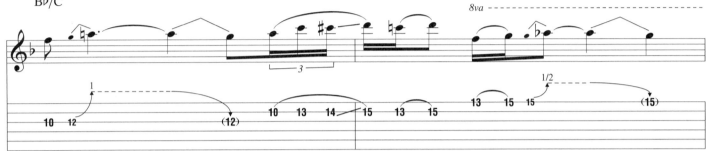

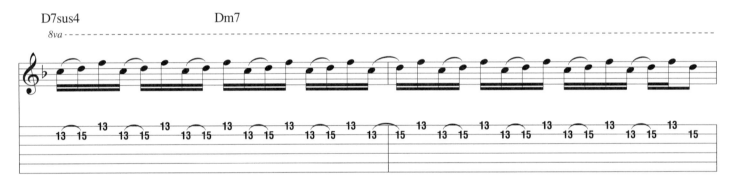

D.S. al Coda

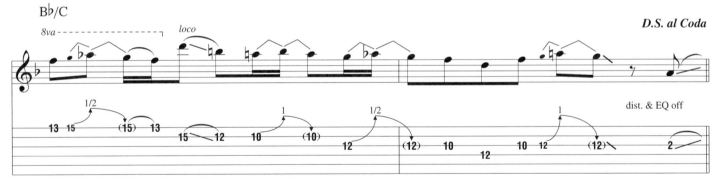

dist. & EQ off

Coda

Bass Solo

Gtr. tacet

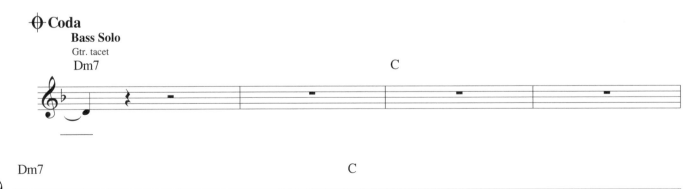

Chorus

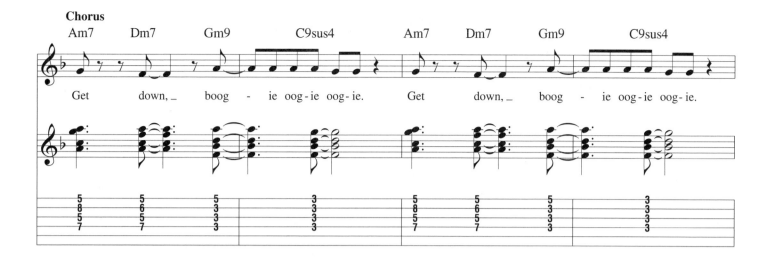

Chorus

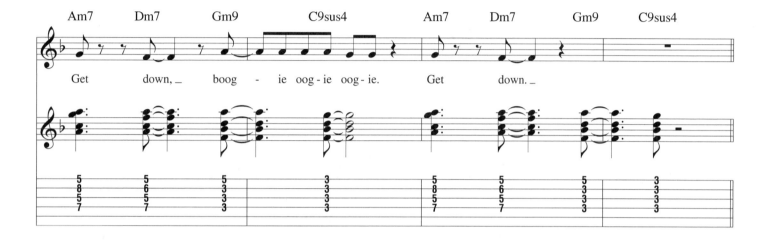

Outro

Repeat and fade

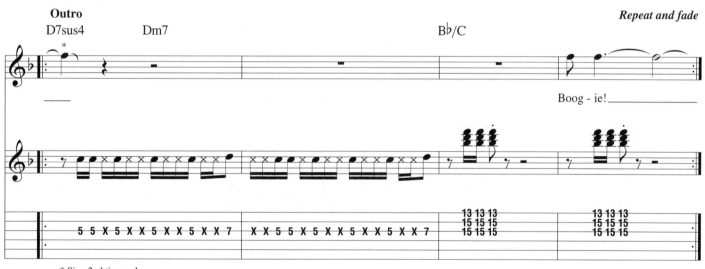

* Sing 2nd time only.

Additional Lyrics

2. There's no time to waste, let's get this show on the road.
Listen to the music and let your body flow.
The sooner we begin, the longer we've got to groove.
Listen to the music and let your body move.

Chorus Now get on up on the floor
'Cause we're gonna boogie oogie oogie
Till we just can't boogie no more, boogie no more.
You can't boogie no more, boogie no more.
Listen to my bass, yeah.

Get Down Tonight

Words and Music by Harry Wayne Casey and Richard Finch

Intro
Moderate Disco ♩ = 116

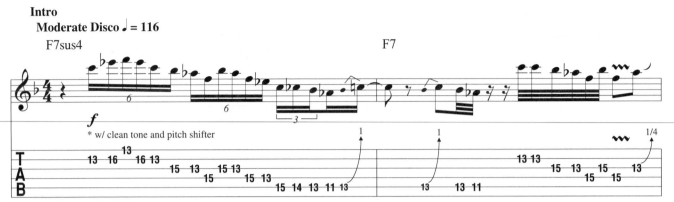

* w/ clean tone and pitch shifter

* This solo was recorded at half speed and then sped up on the original recording, causing it to sound one octave higher. Use a pitch shifter or whammy pedal set for one octave up to create this sound.

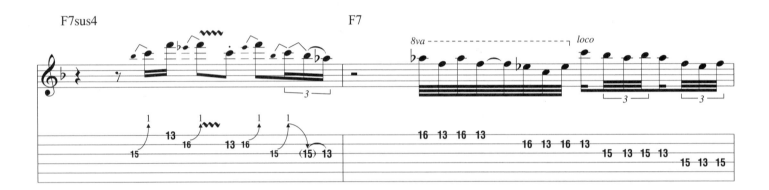

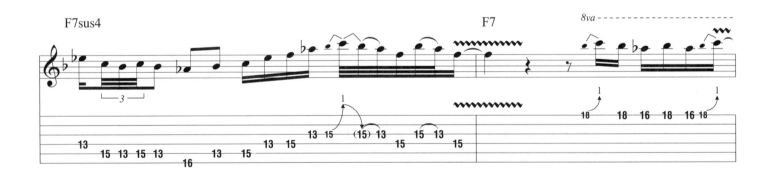

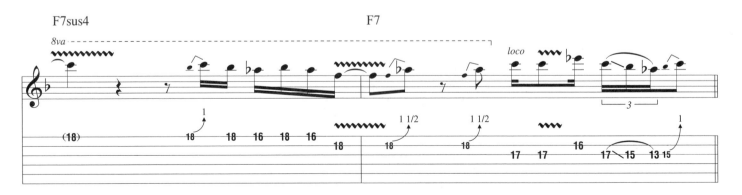

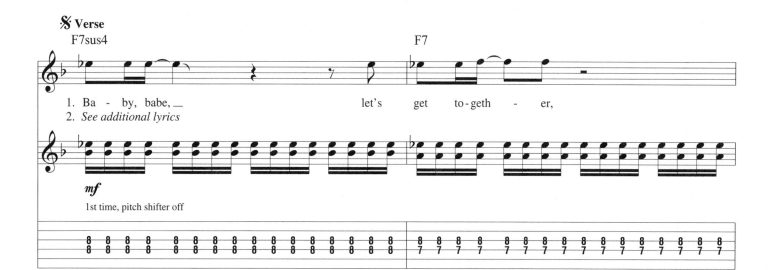

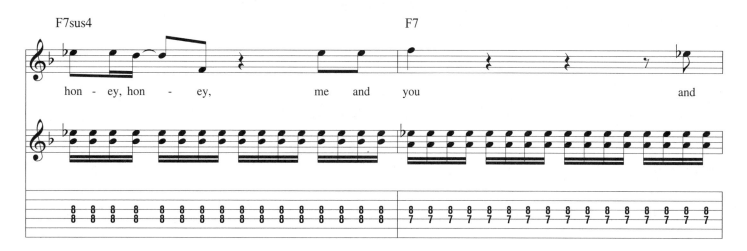

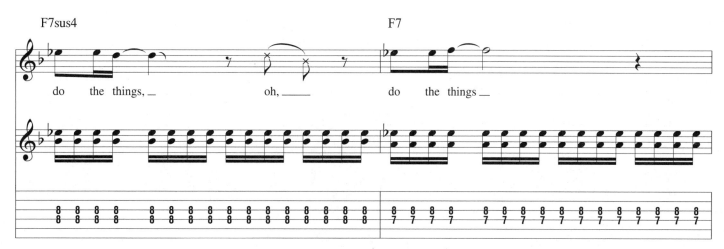

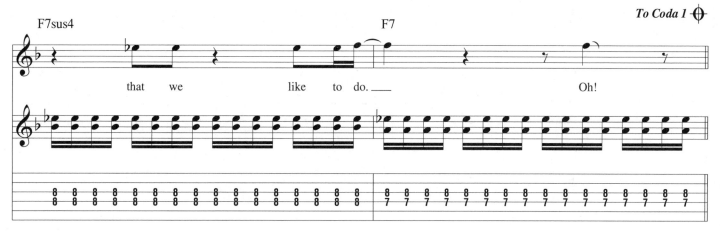

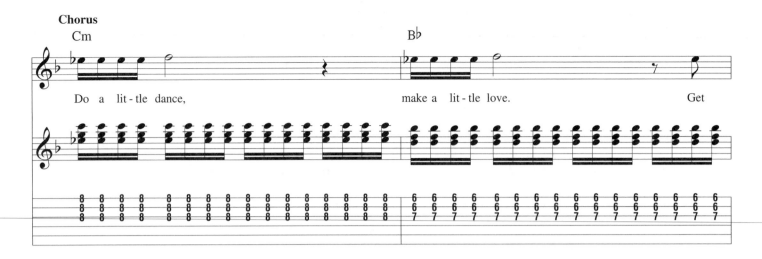

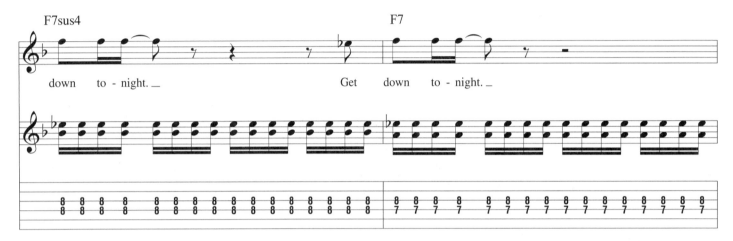

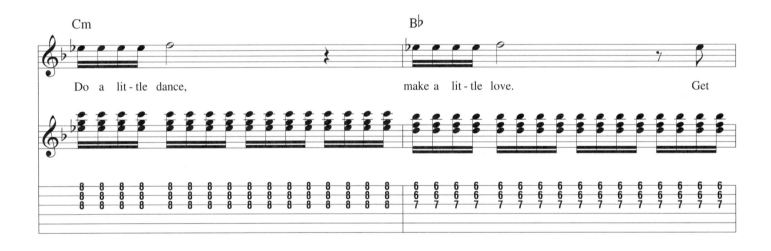

D.S. al Coda 1

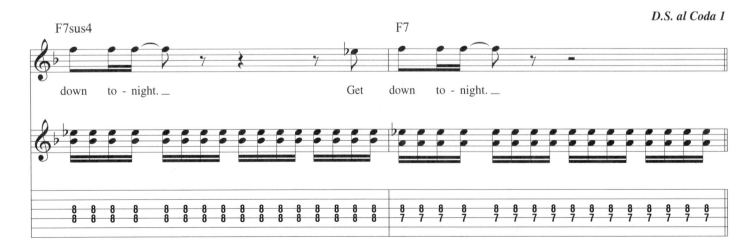

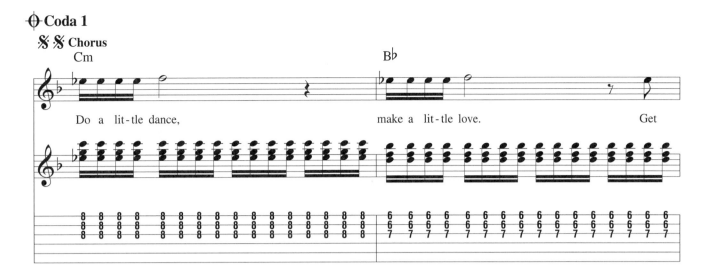

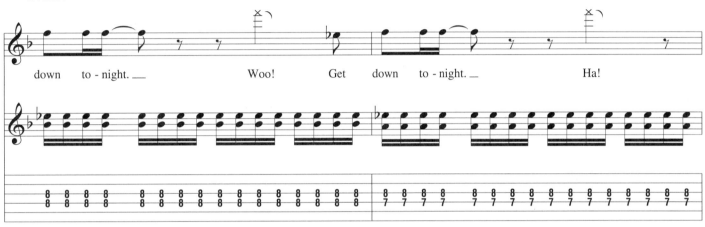

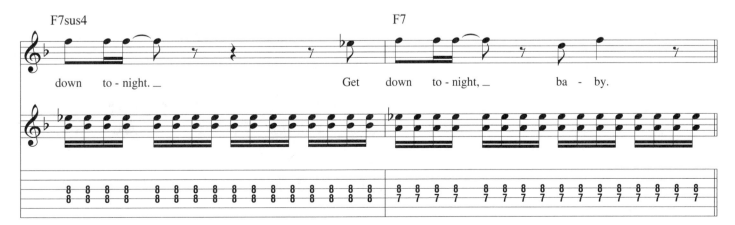

Guitar Solo

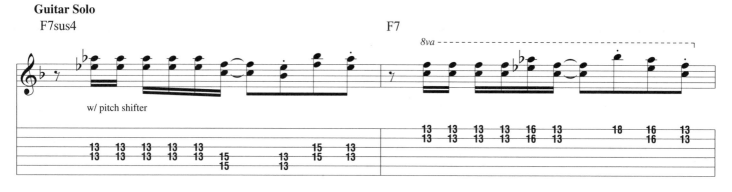

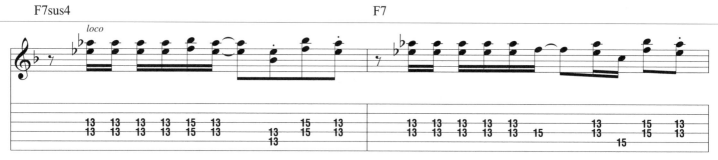

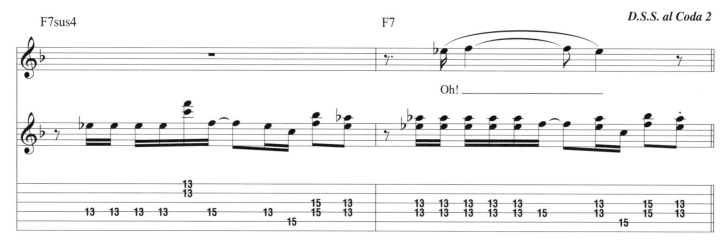

Coda 2

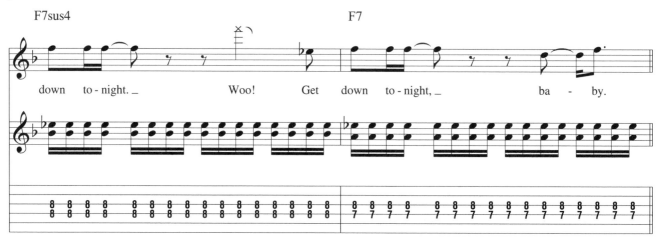

Interlude

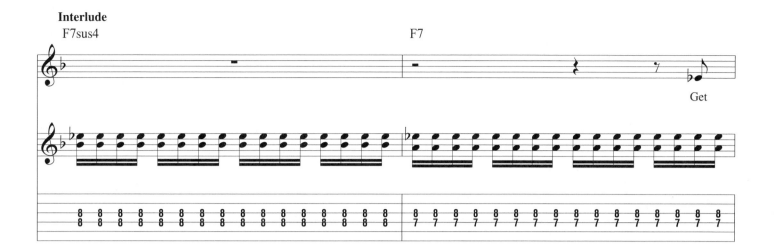

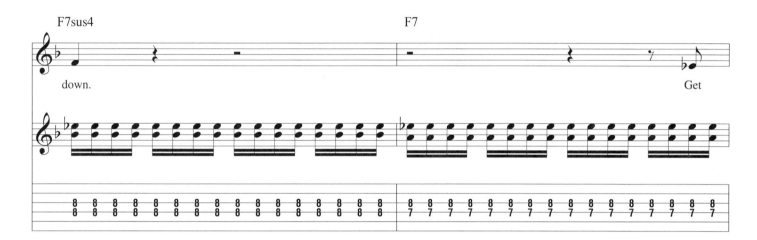

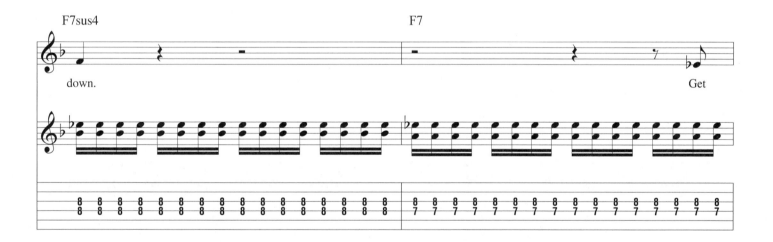

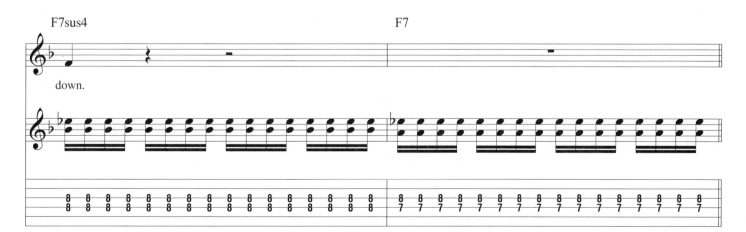

Outro

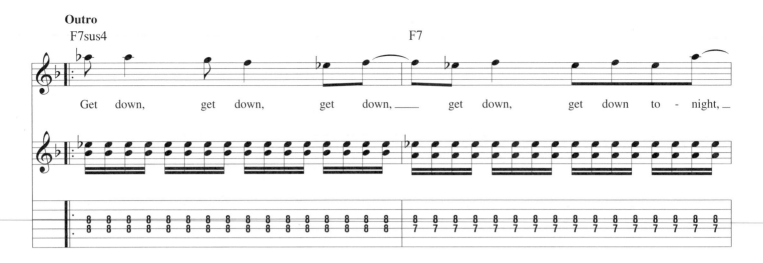

Get down, get down, get down, get down, get down to - night, ___

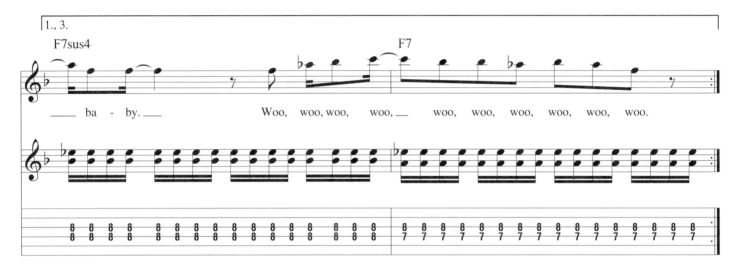

___ ba - by. ___ Woo, woo, woo, woo, ___ woo, woo, woo, woo, woo, woo.

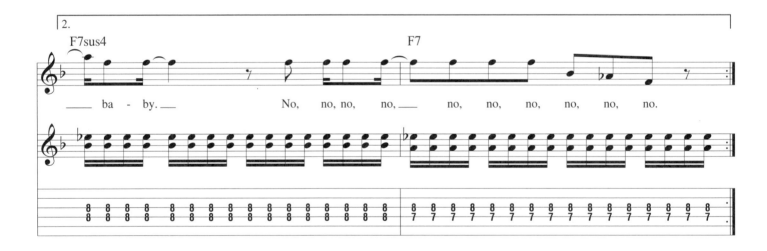

___ ba - by. ___ No, no, no, no, ___ no, no, no, no, no, no.

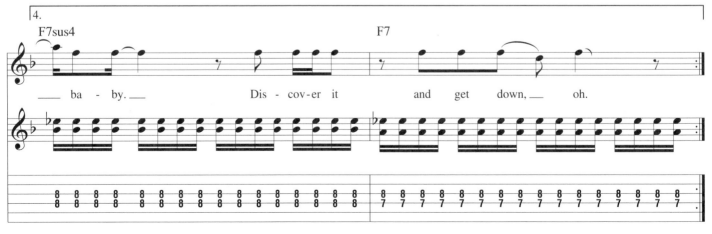

___ ba - by. ___ Dis - cov-er it and get down, ___ oh.

18

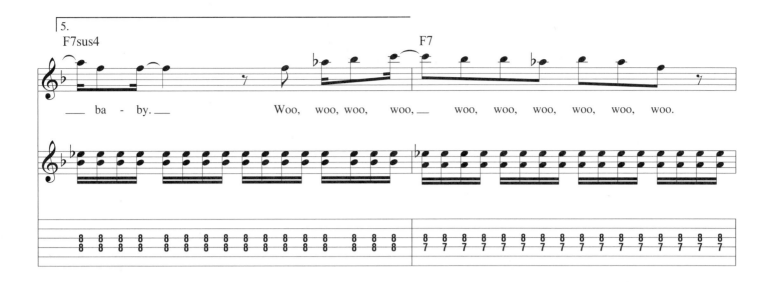

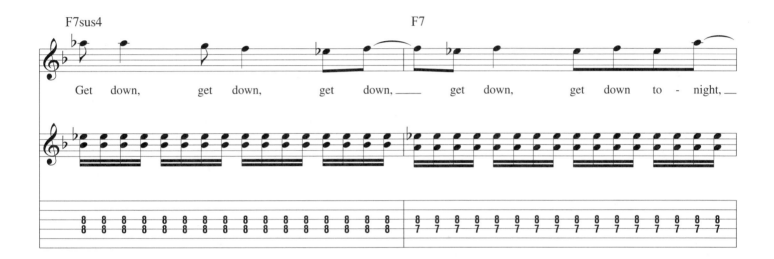

Begin fade   **Fade out**

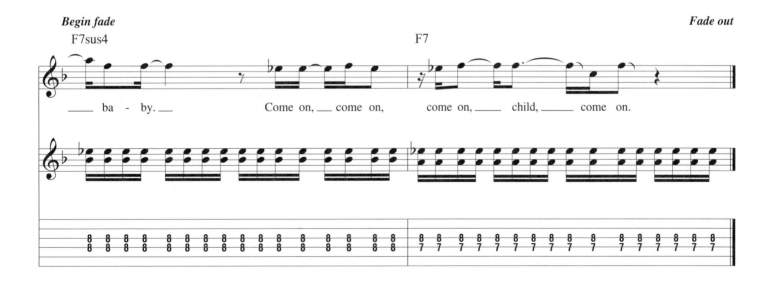

Additional Lyrics

2. Baby, babe,
   I'll meet you some place, some time,
   Where we can, oh, get together
   And ease up our mind. Oh!

Hot Stuff

Words and Music by Pete Bellotte, Harold Faltermeyer and Keith Forsey

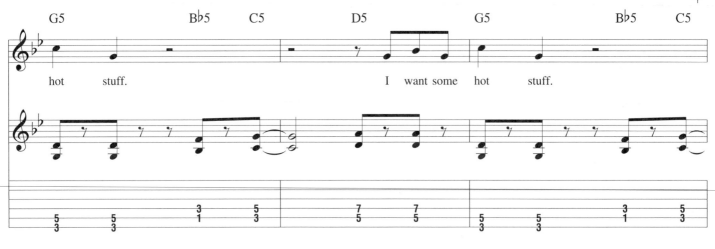

hot stuff.   I want some hot stuff.

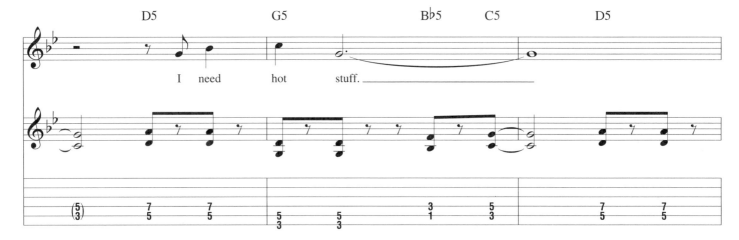

I need hot stuff. _____

Interlude

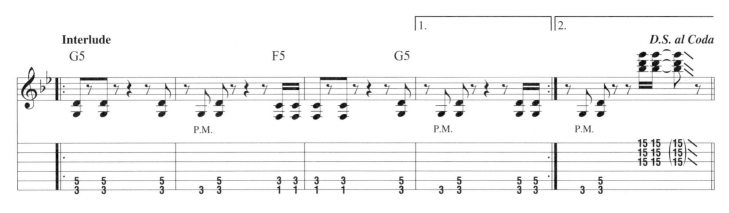

D.S. al Coda

 Coda

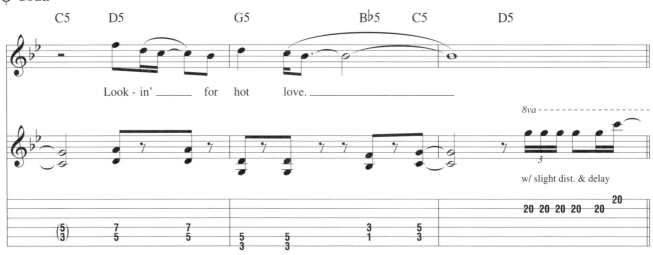

Look - in' _____ for hot love. _____

w/ slight dist. & delay

Guitar Solo

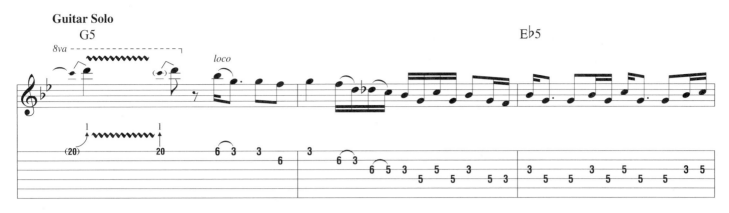

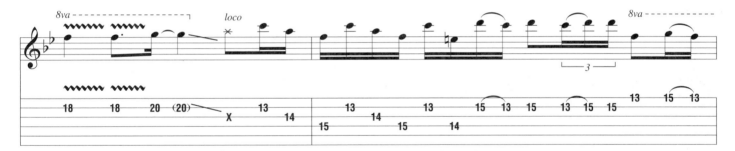

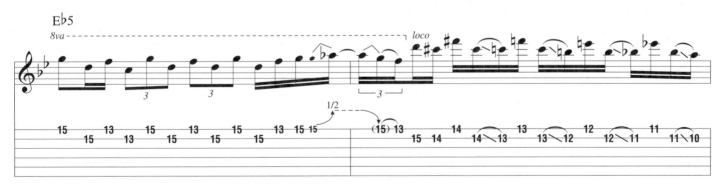

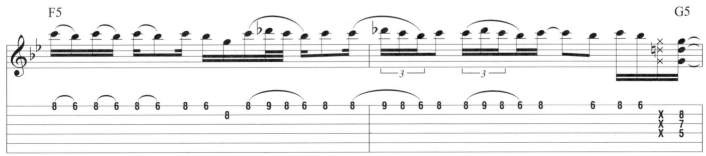

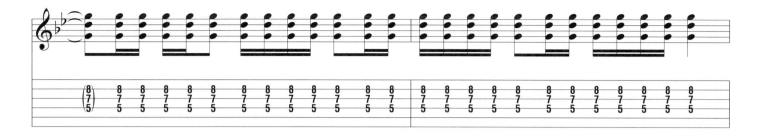

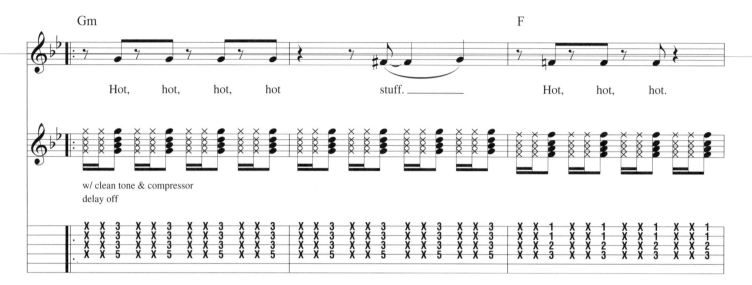

Hot, hot, hot, hot stuff. _____ Hot, hot, hot.

w/ clean tone & compressor
delay off

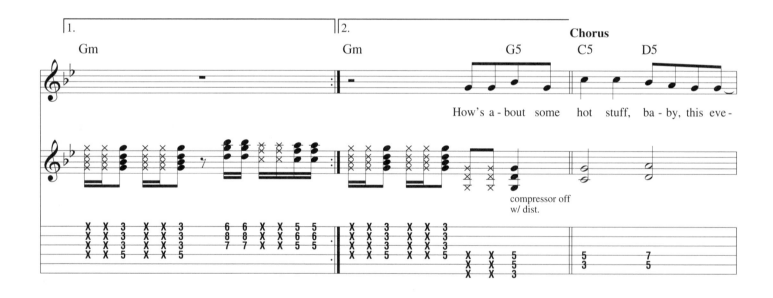

1.

Gm

2.

Gm

Chorus

G5   C5   D5

How's a - bout some hot stuff, ba - by, this eve -

compressor off
w/ dist.

G5

F5 G5   C5   D5

G5

F5 G5

- nin'? _____ I need some hot stuff, ba - by, to - night. _____ Look - in' for my

P.M.

P.M.

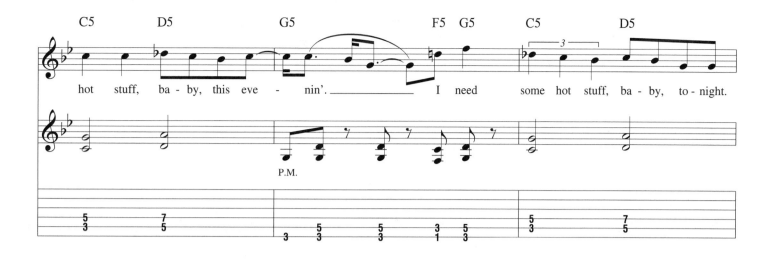

Outro

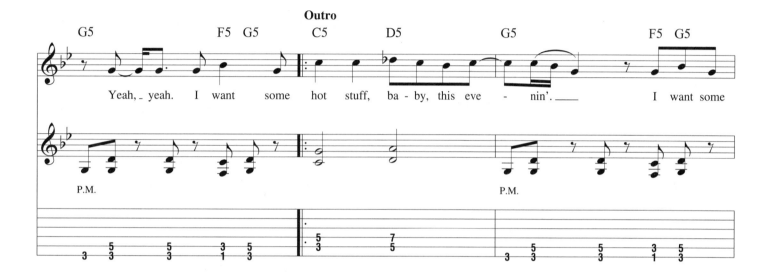

Repeat and fade

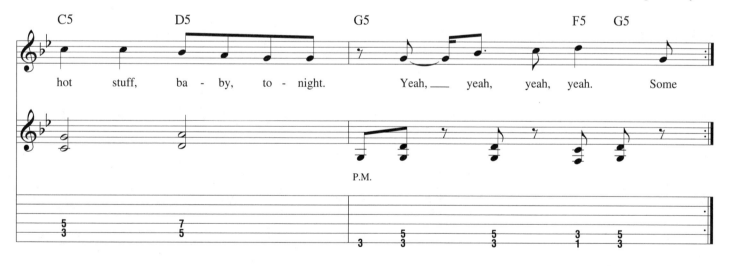

Additional Lyrics

2. Lookin' for a lover who needs another,
   Don't want another night on my own.
   Want to share my love with a warm-blooded lover.
   Want to bring a wild man back home.

Chorus Gotta have some hot love, baby, this evenin'.
   I need some hot stuff, baby, tonight.
   I want some hot stuff, baby, this evenin'.
   Gotta have some lovin'. Got to have love tonight.
   I need hot stuff. Hot love. Lookin' for hot love.

I Will Survive

Words and Music by Dino Fekaris and Frederick J. Perren

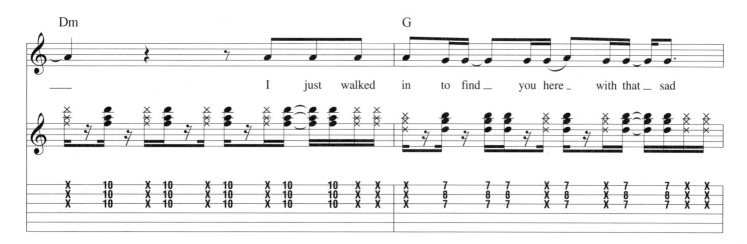

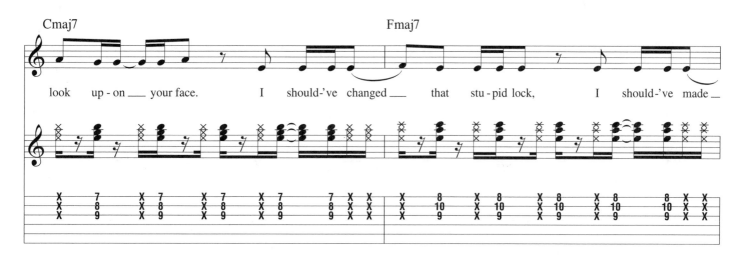

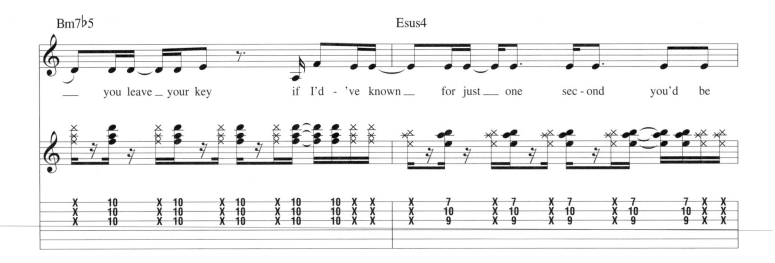

Bm7♭5 ... **Esus4**

_you leave _ your key _ if I'd - 've known _ for just _ one sec - ond you'd be

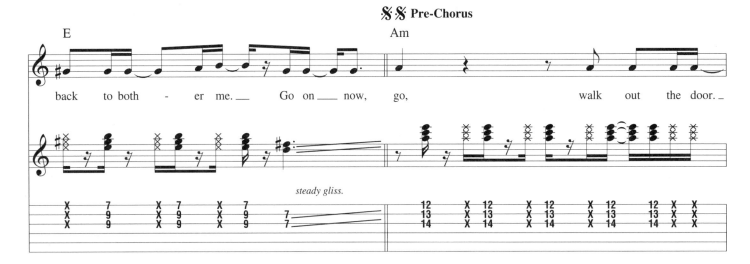

𝄋 𝄋 **Pre-Chorus**

E ... **Am**

back to both - er me. _ Go on _ now, go, walk out the door. _

steady gliss.

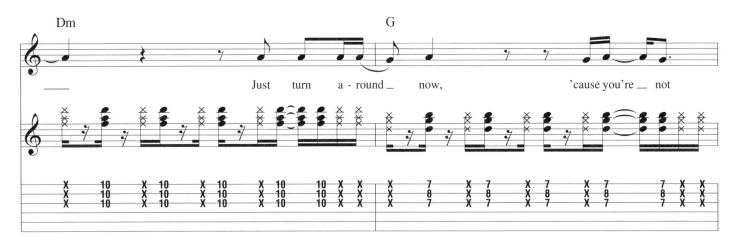

Dm ... **G**

_ Just turn a - round _ now, 'cause you're _ not

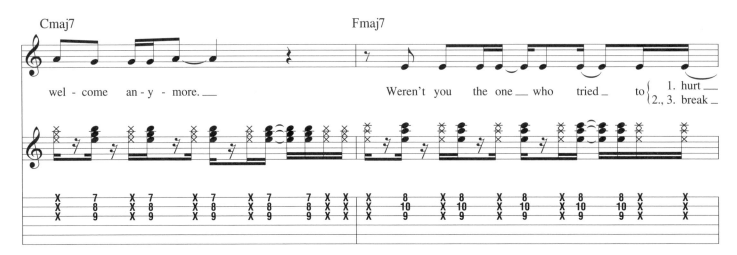

Cmaj7 ... **Fmaj7**

wel - come an - y - more. _ Weren't you the one _ who tried _ to { 1. hurt
2., 3. break _

28

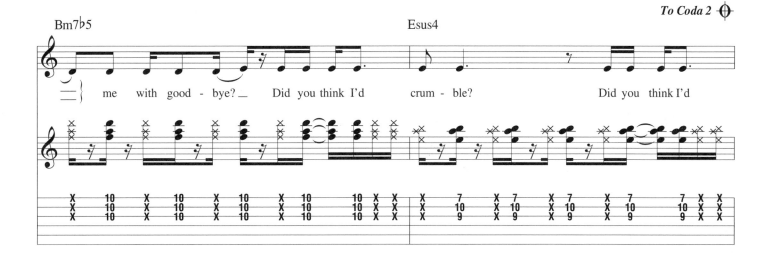

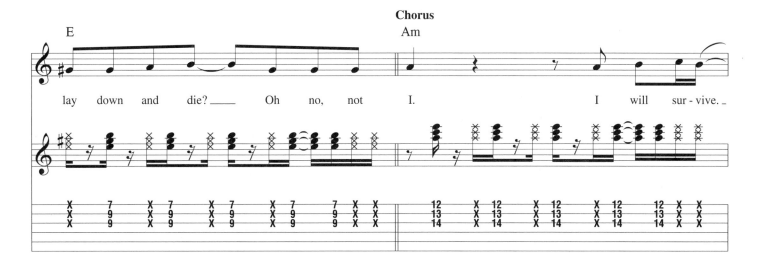

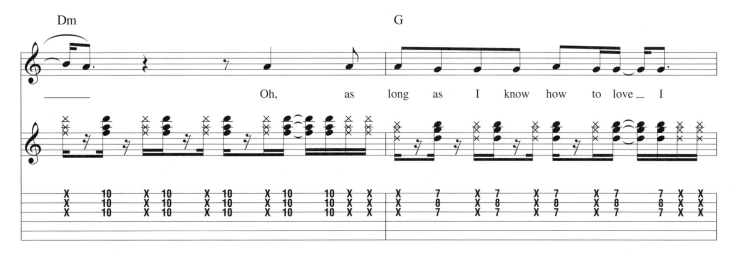

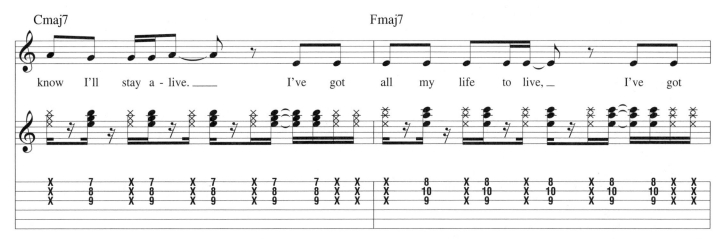

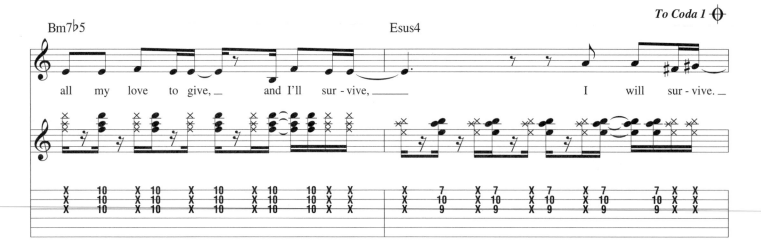

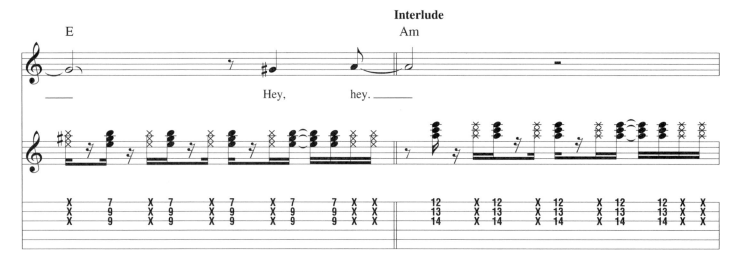

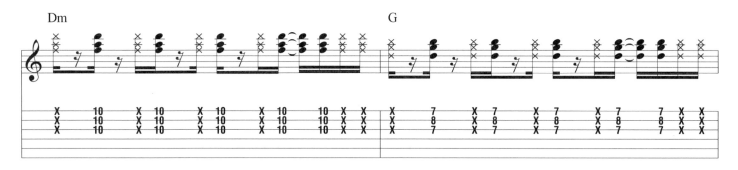

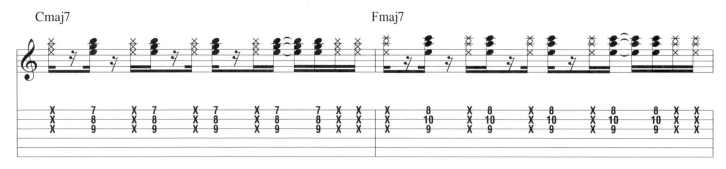

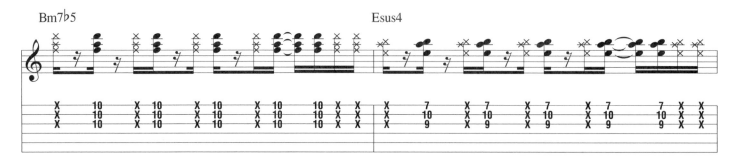

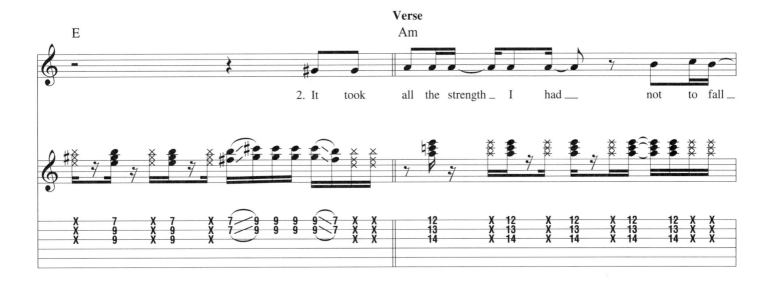

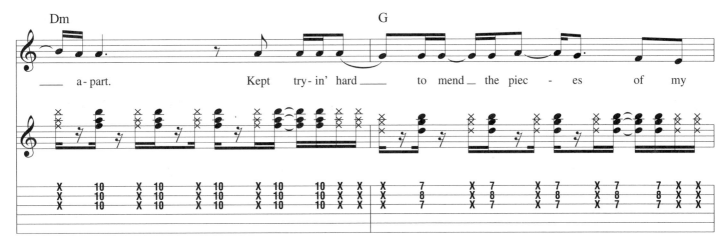

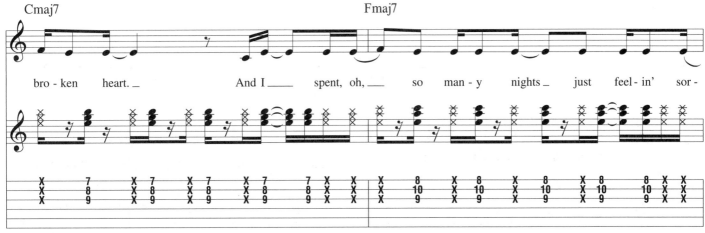

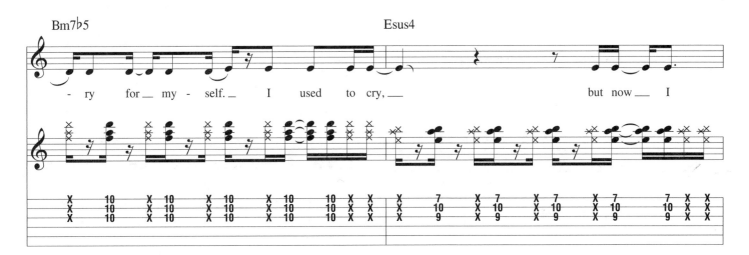

D.S. al Coda 1

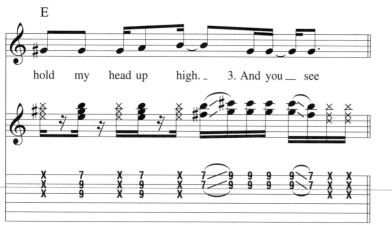

hold my head up high. __ 3. And you __ see

Coda 1

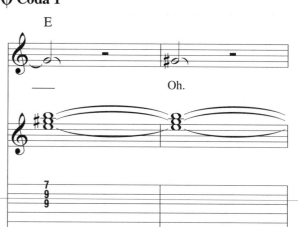

Oh.

D.S.S. al Coda 2

Go on, __ now,

Coda 2

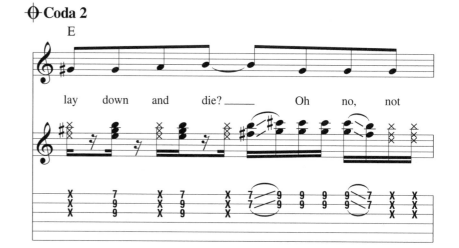

lay down and die? _____ Oh no, not

Chorus   **Begin fade**

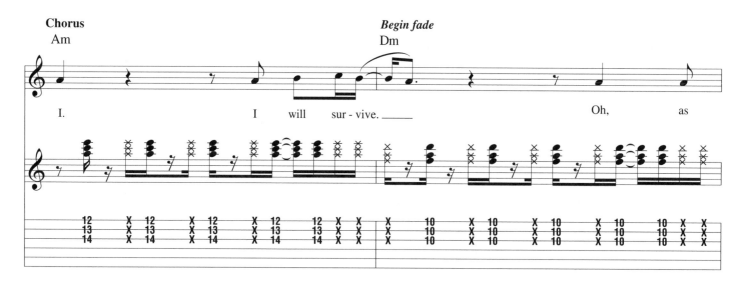

I.   I will sur-vive. _____   Oh, as

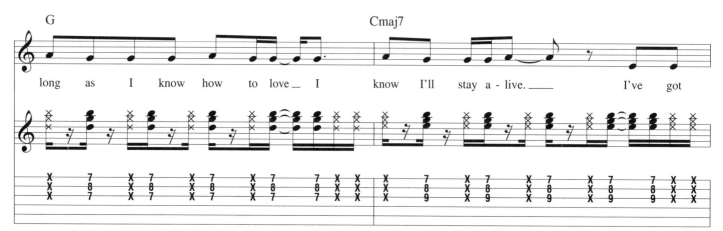

long as I know how to love __ I   know I'll stay a-live. _____   I've got

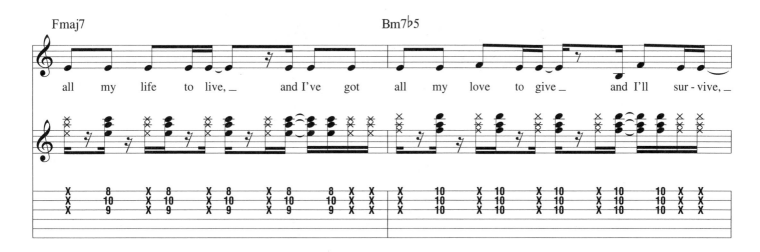

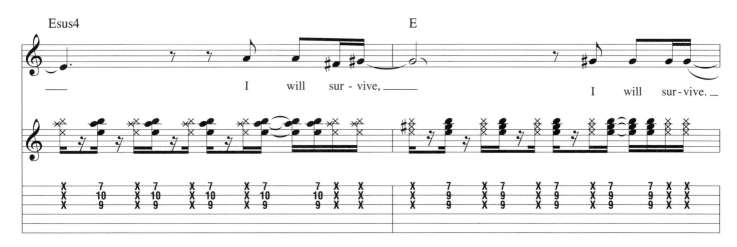

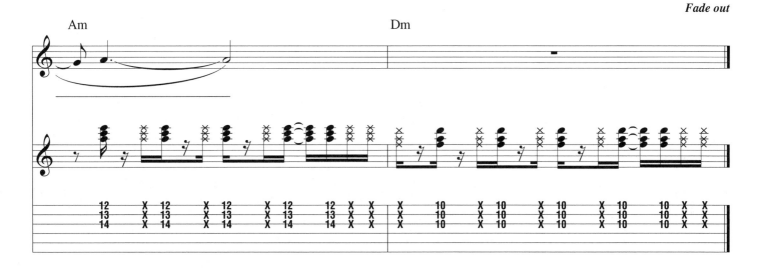

Additional Lyrics

3. And you see me, somebody new.
   I'm not that chained up little person
   Still in love with you.
   And so you felt like droppin' in
   And just expect me to be free.
   But now I'm savin' all my lovin'
   For someone who's lovin' me.

Love Rollercoaster

**Words and Music by Ralph Middlebrooks, James Williams, Marshall Jones,
Leroy Bonner, Clarence Satchell, William Beck and Marvin Pierce**

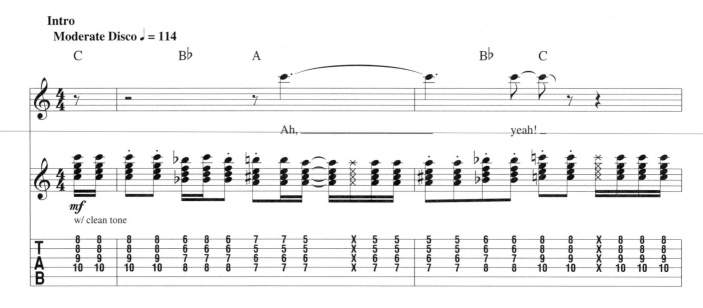

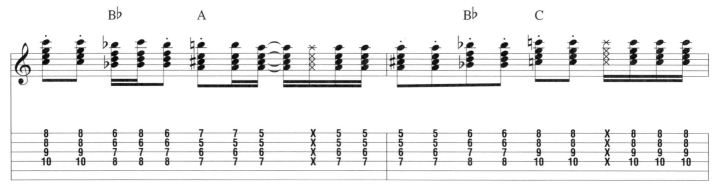

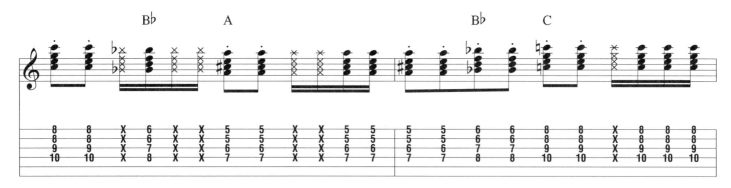

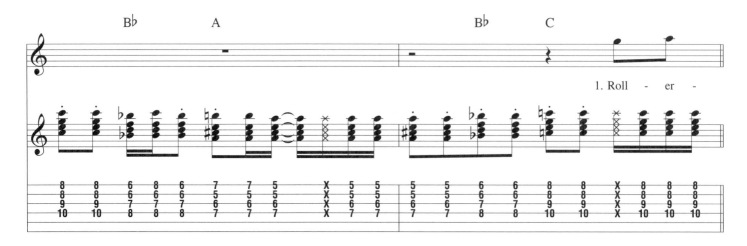

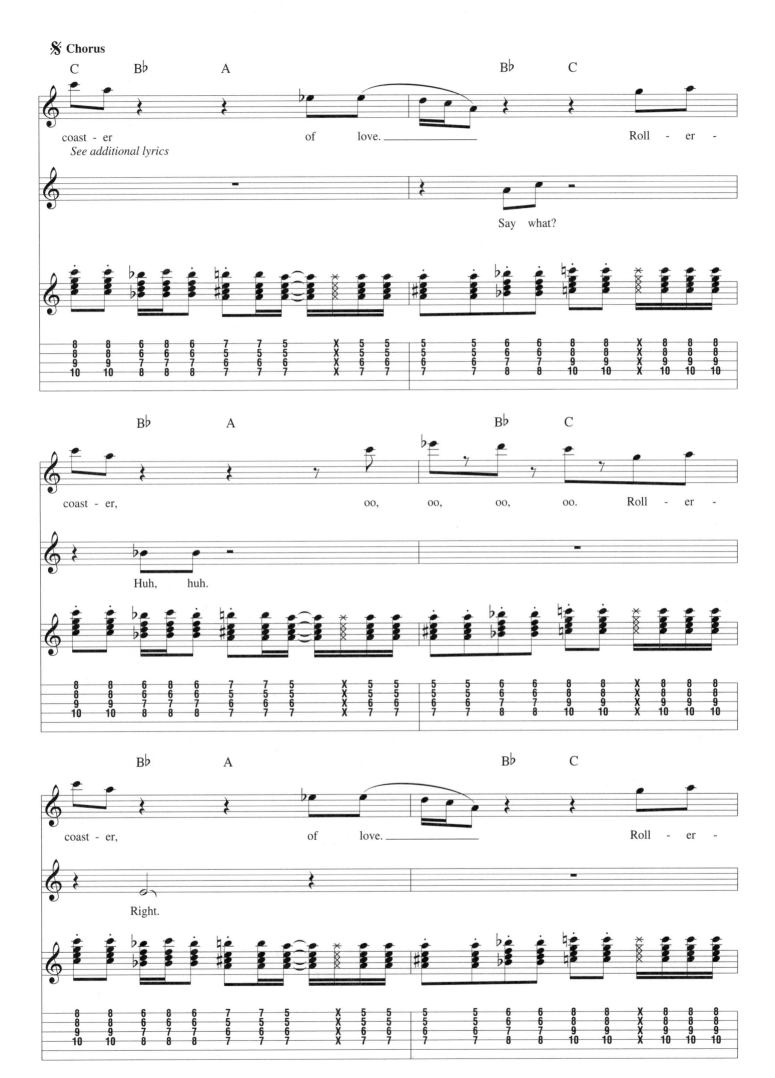

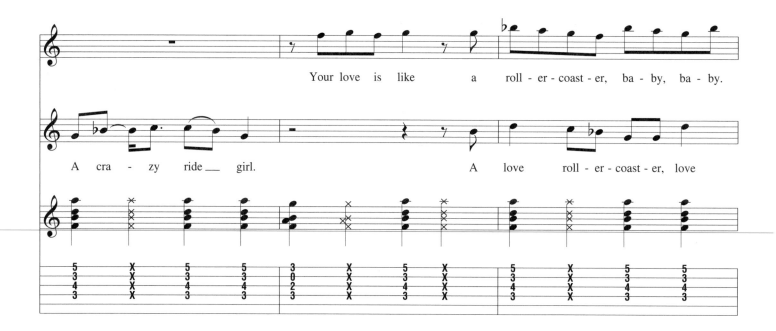

Your love is like a roll-er-coast-er, ba-by, ba-by.

A cra-zy ride __ girl. A love roll-er-coast-er, love

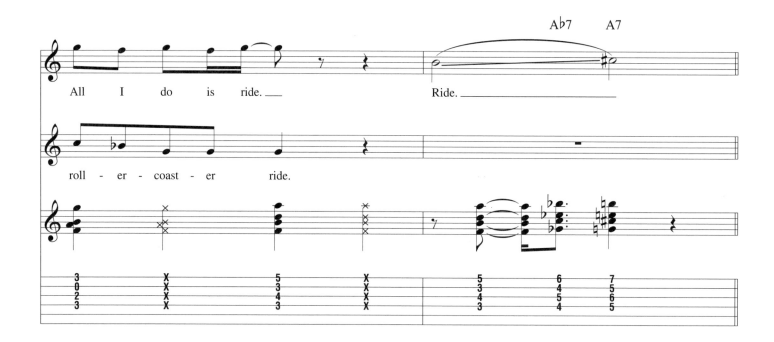

Ab7   A7

All I do is ride. __ Ride. __

roll-er-coast-er ride.

Interlude

C   Bb   A   Bb   C

Huh, huh.

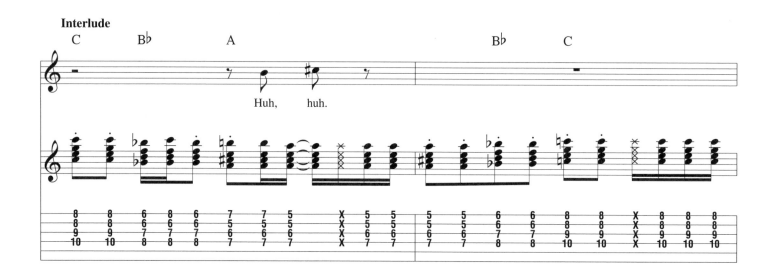

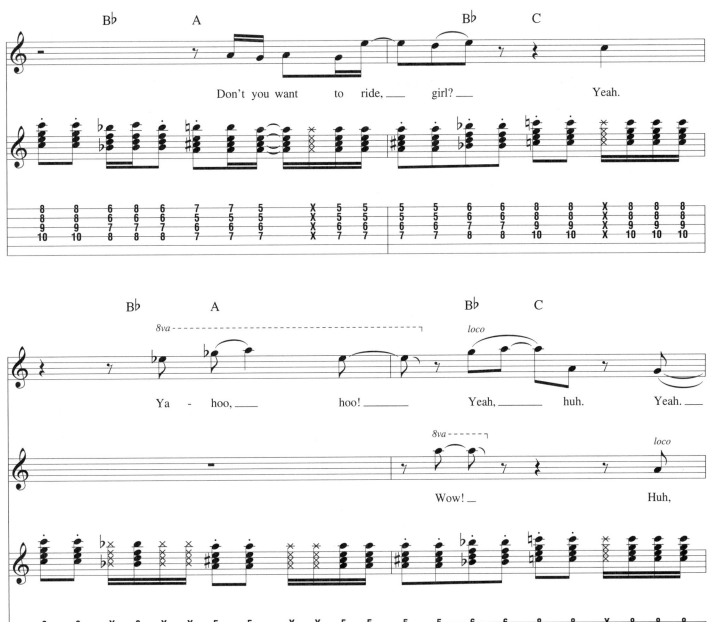

Don't you want   to ride, ___ girl? ___   Yeah.

Ya - hoo, ___   hoo! _____   Yeah, _____ huh.   Yeah. ___

Wow! __   Huh,

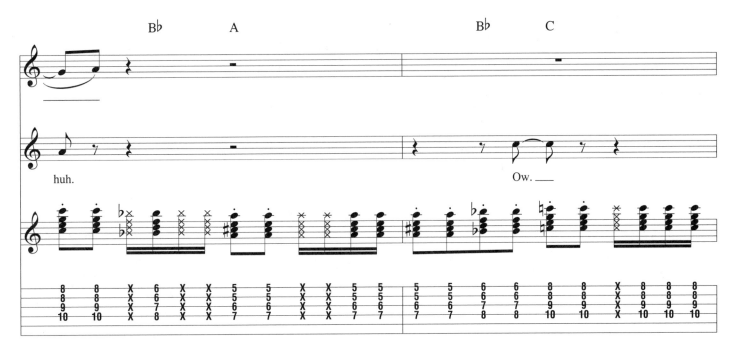

huh.   Ow. ___

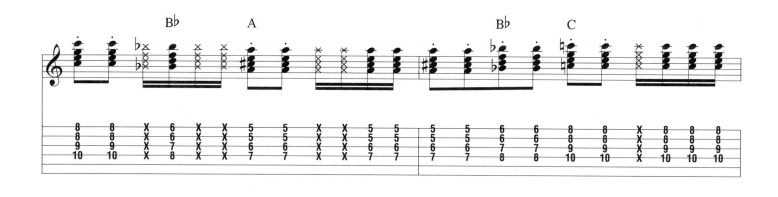

D.S. al Coda

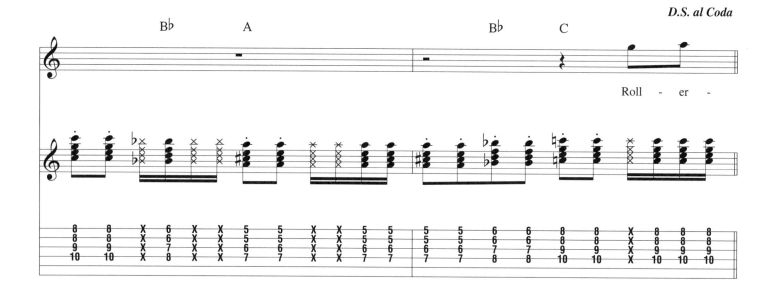

Roll - er -

Your love is like a roll - er - coast - er, ba - by, ba - by.

Love roll - er - coast - er, love

roll - er - coast - er, ba - by, ba - by. All I do is ride. _

Your love is like a roll - er - coast - er, ba - by, ba - by. All I do is ride. _

Love, _____ love _____ roll - er - coast - er, girl. Right.

Ride, _ ride, _ ride. _____ Ride on the roll - er - coast - er, ba - by, ba - by.

Hey. Right. _

Additional Lyrics

Chorus   Love rollercoaster, girl. Huh.
        Lovin' you in a crazy world, child. Huh.
        Let me ride one more time.
        High, high, high, high now.
        Oh. High.

Super Freak

Words and Music by Rick James and Alonzo Miller

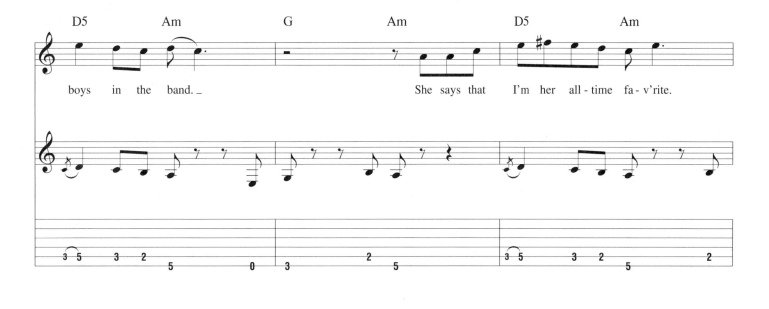

boys in the band. ___ She says that I'm her all - time fa - v'rite.

When I make my move to her room it's the right time. She's

Pre-Chorus

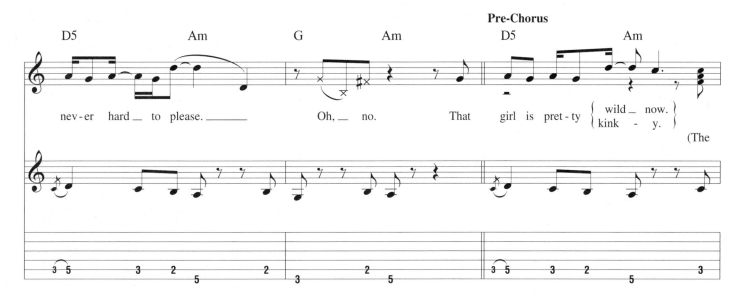

nev - er hard ___ to please. _____ Oh, ___ no. That girl is pret - ty { wild ___ now. } { kink - y. }

(The

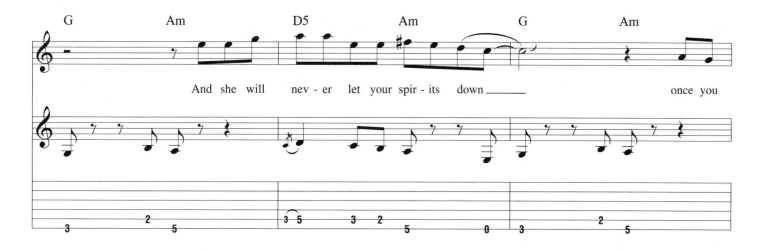

And she will nev-er let your spir-its down _____ once you

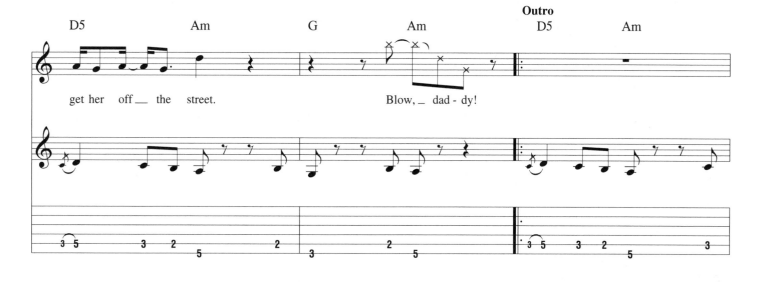

Outro

get her off __ the street.   Blow, __ dad-dy!

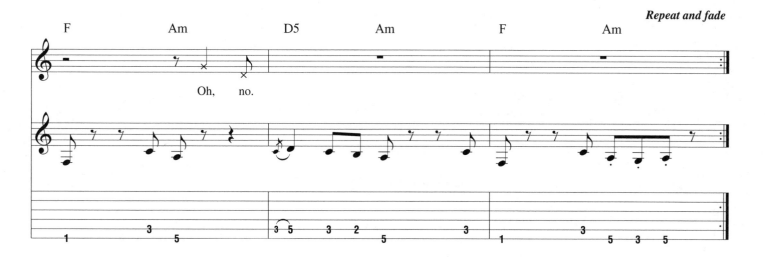

Repeat and fade

Oh,   no.

Additional Lyrics

2. She's a very special girl (The kind of girl you want to love.)
   From her head down to her toenails. (Down to her feet, yeah.)
   And she'll wait for me backstage with her girlfriends
   In a limousine. (Long and black and shining bright.)
   Three's not a crowd to her. She says, (Ménage à trois, we love you.)
   "Room 714, I'll be waiting."
   When I get there she's got incense, wine and candles.
   It's such a freaky scene.

49

We Are Family

Words and Music by Nile Rodgers and Bernard Edwards

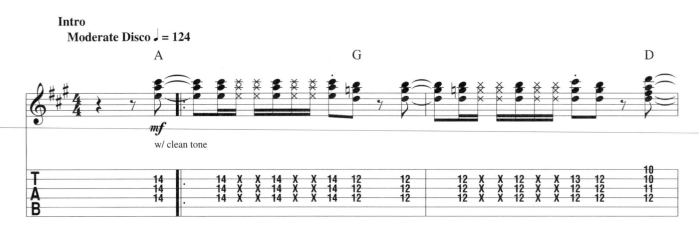

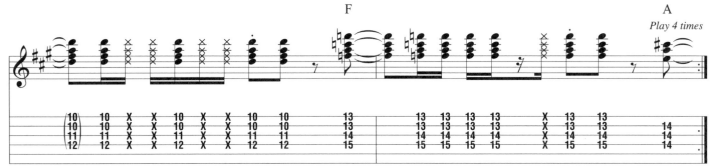

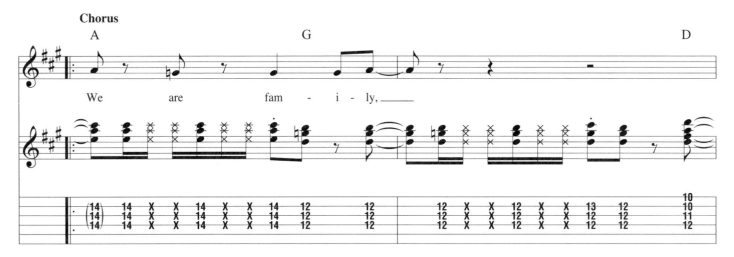

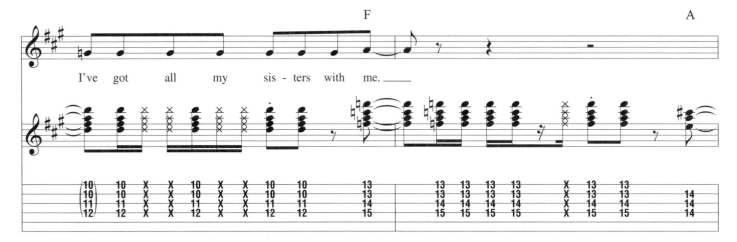

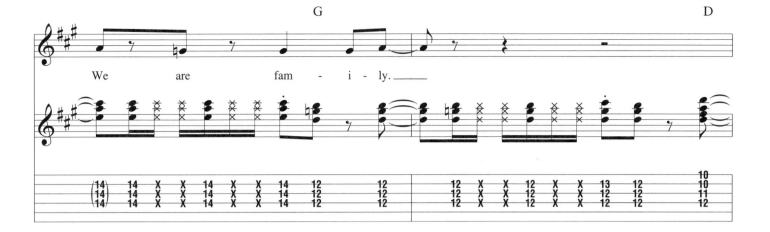

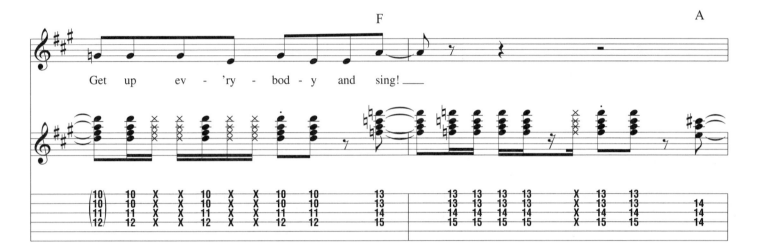

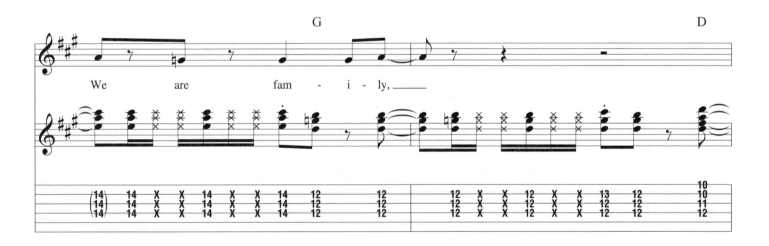

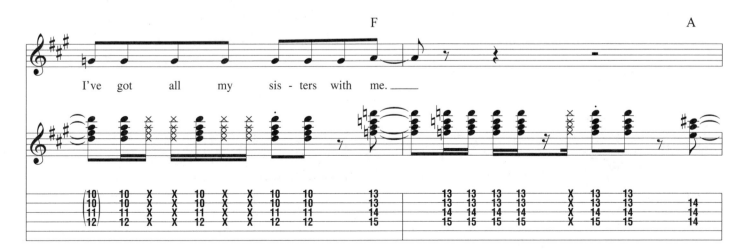

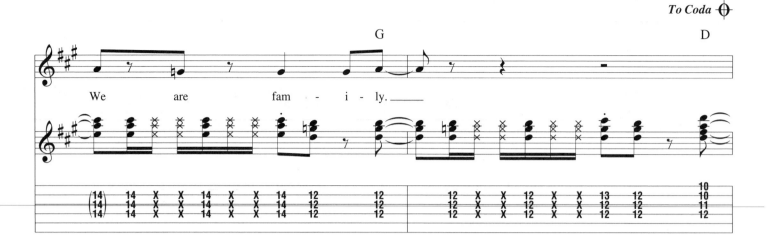

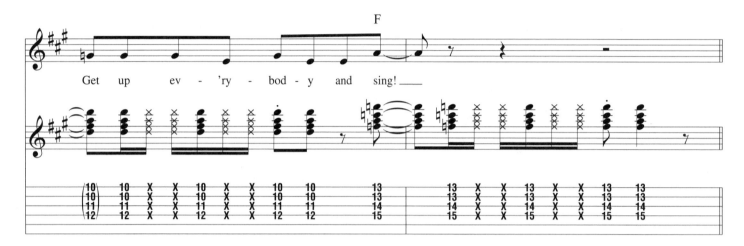

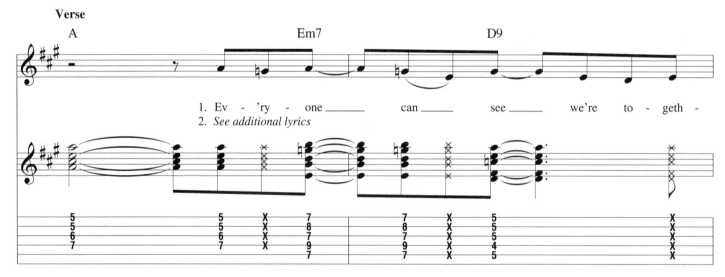

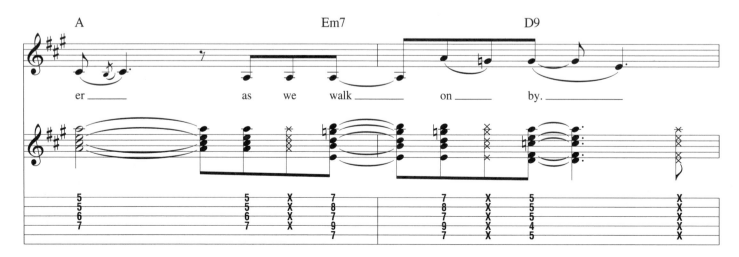

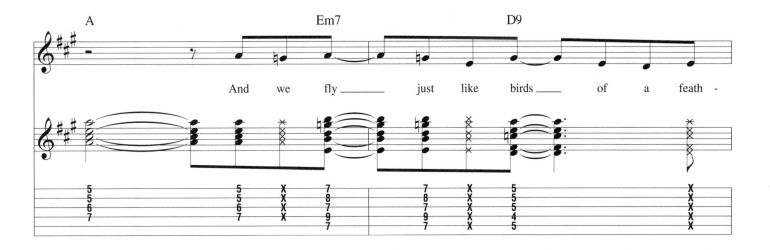

And we fly ____ just like birds ____ of a feath -

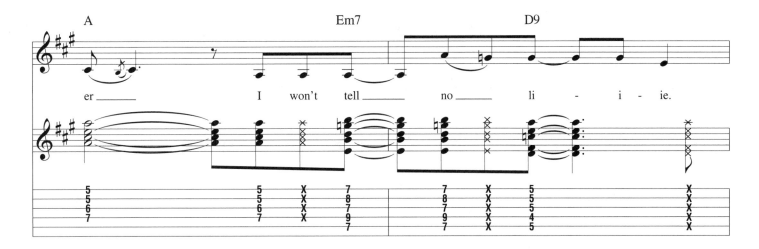

er ____ I won't tell _____ no _____ li - i - ie.

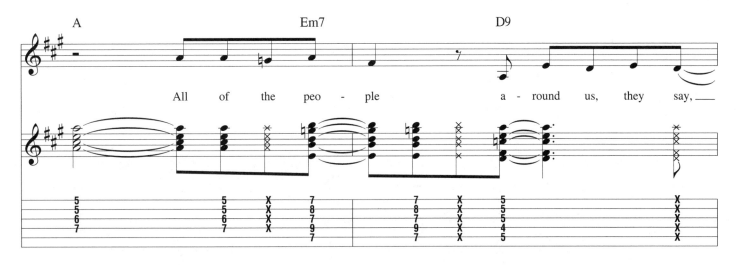

All of the peo - ple a - round us, they say, ___

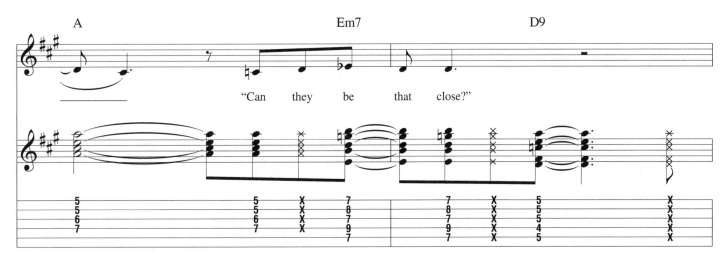

"Can they be that close?"

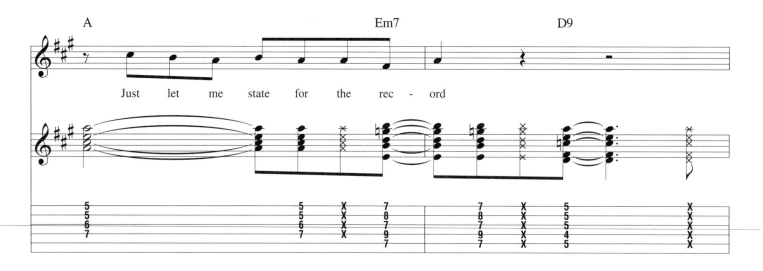

2nd time, D.S. al Coda

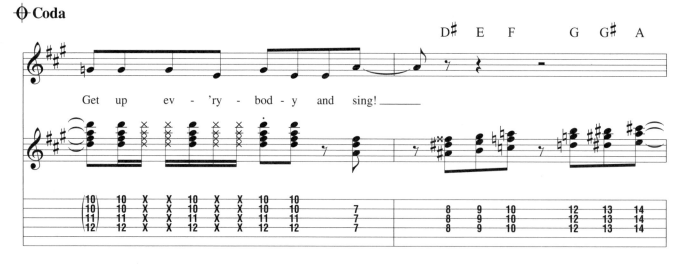

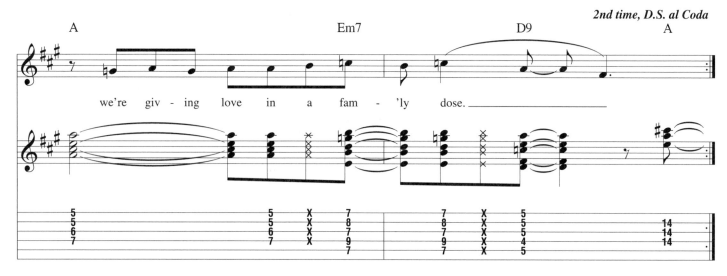

Coda

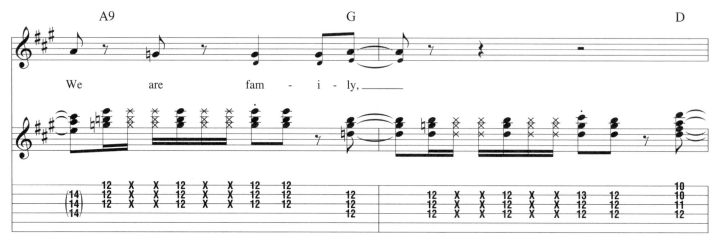

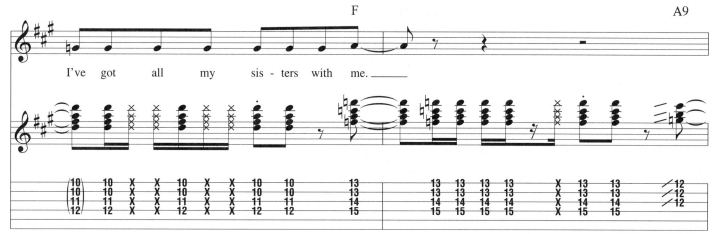

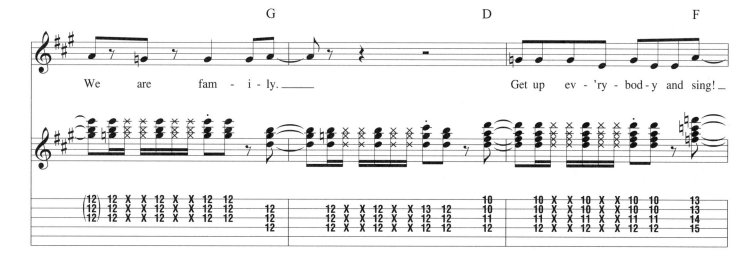

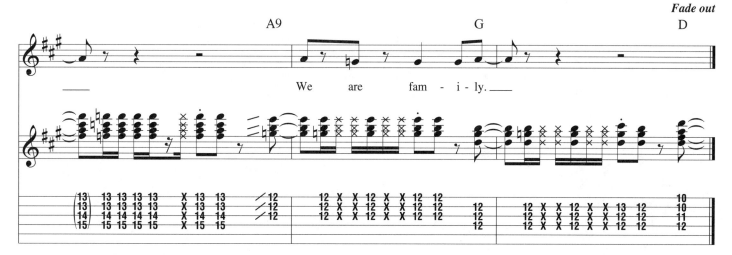

Additional Lyrics

2. Living life is fun and we've just begun
   To get our share of this world's delights.
   High hopes we have for the future
   And our goal's in sight.
   No, we don't get depressed,
   Here's what we call our golden rule:
   Have faith in you and the things you do,
   You won't go wrong.
   Oh, no. This is our fam'ly jewel.

Stayin' Alive

from the Motion Picture SATURDAY NIGHT FEVER
Words and Music by Barry Gibb, Robin Gibb and Maurice Gibb

Intro
Moderate Disco ♩ = 104

1. Well, you can tell ___

% Verse

___ by the way I use ___ my walk, I'm a wom - an's man, no ___ time to talk. And
2. See additional lyrics

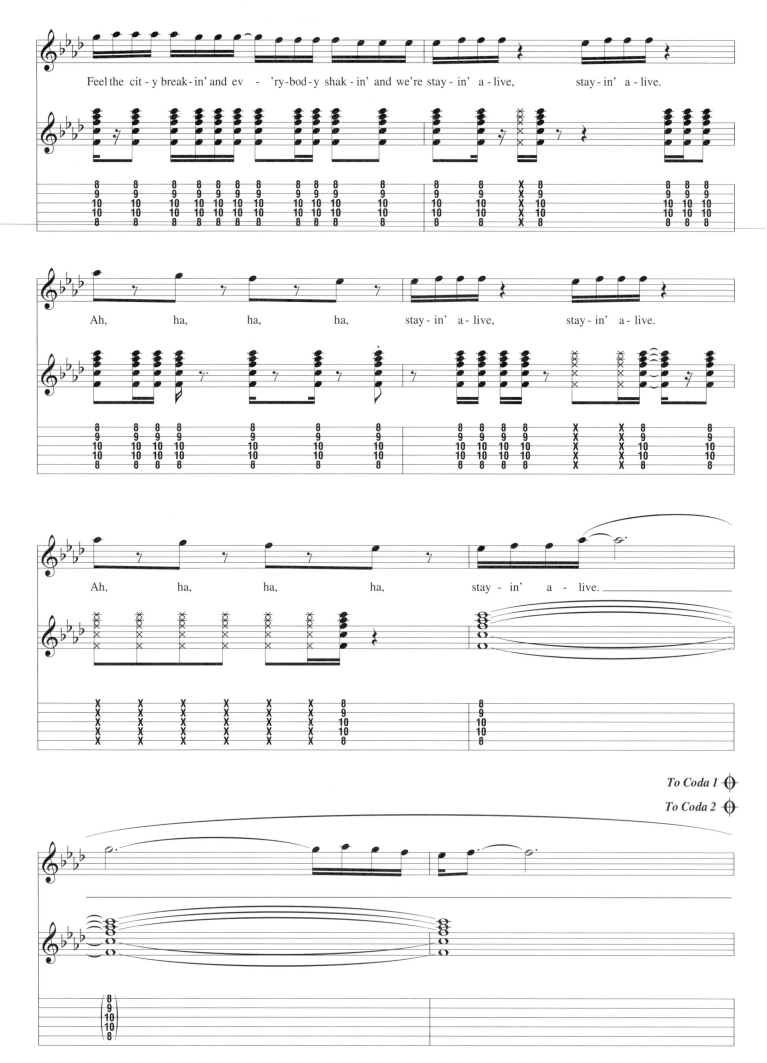

To Coda 1

To Coda 2

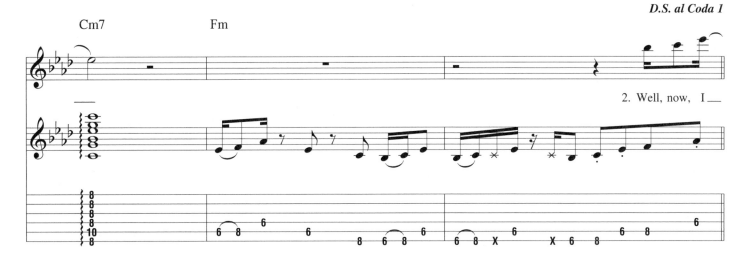

2. Well, now, I

Coda 1

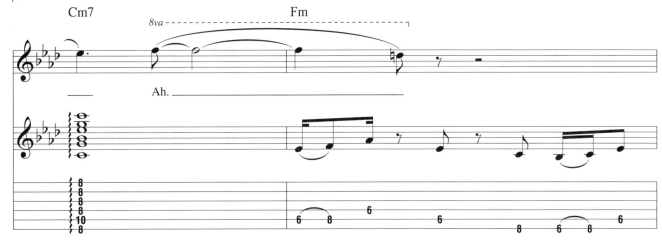

Ah.

Bridge

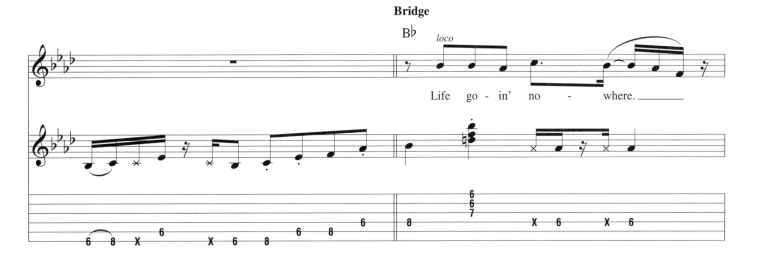

Life go - in' no - where.

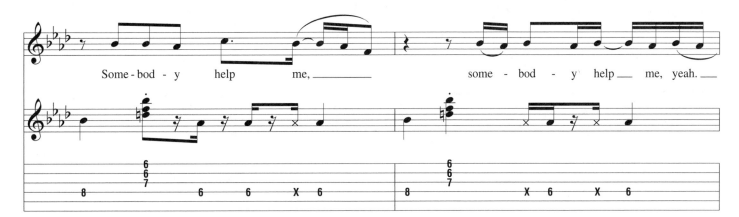

Some - bod - y help me, some - bod - y help me, yeah.

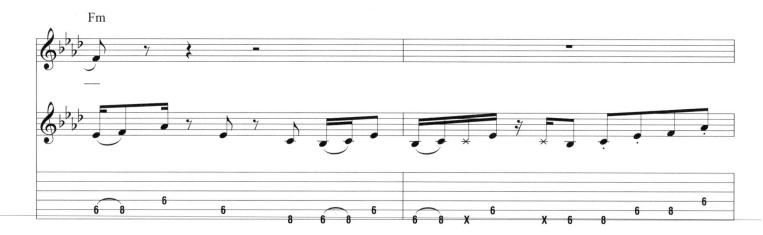

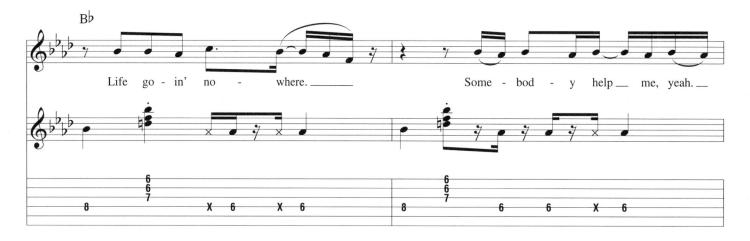

Life go-in' no - where. _____ Some - bod - y help _ me, yeah. _____

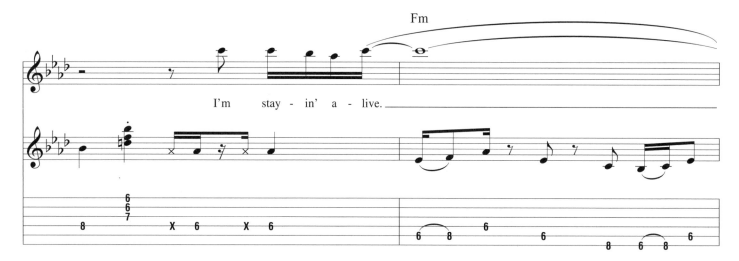

I'm stay - in' a - live. _____

D.S. al Coda 2
(take 1st lyrics)

3. Well, you can tell _____

Coda 2

Cm7

_____ Oh,

yeah. ___

Outro

Life go - in' no - where. _____ Some-bod - y help ___ me _____

Some - bod - y help ___ me, yeah. _____ Yeah.

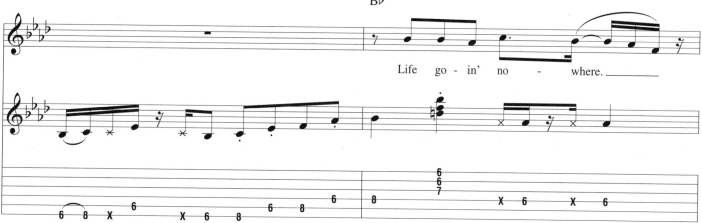

Life go - in' no - where. _____

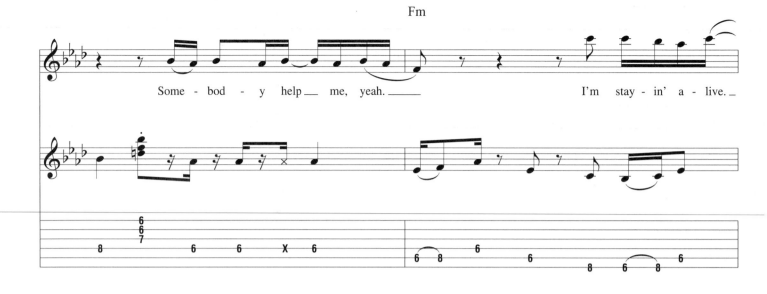

Fm

Some - bod - y help __ me, yeah. __ I'm stay - in' a - live. __

Play 4 times and fade

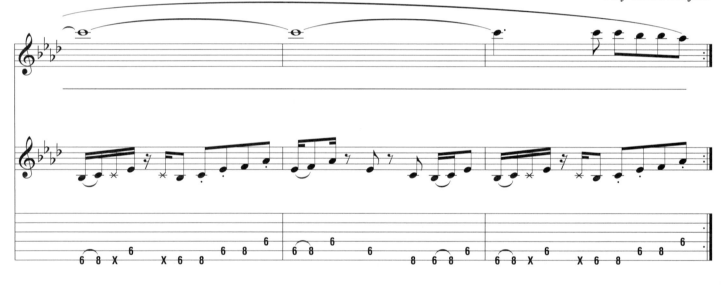

Additional Lyrics

2. Well, now, I get low, and I get high,
   And if I can't get either, I really try.
   Got the wings of heaven on my shoes.
   I'm a dancin' man, and I just can't lose.

Pre-Chorus 2. You know it's alright. It's O.K.
   I'll live to see another day.
   Oh, we can try to understand
   The *New York Times'* effect on man.

Pre-Chorus 3. And now it's alright. It's O.K.
   And you may look the other way.
   Oh, we can try to understand
   The *New York Times'* effect on man.

HAL•LEONARD GUITAR PLAY-ALONG®

This series will help you play your favorite songs quickly and easily. **INCLUDES TAB**
Just follow the tab and listen to the CD to hear how the guitar should sound, and then play along using the separate backing tracks. Mac or PC users can also slow down the tempo without changing pitch by using the CD in their computer. The melody and lyrics are included in the book so that you can sing or simply follow along.

VOL. 1 – ROCK	00699570 / $16.99	**VOL. 45 – TV THEMES**	00699718 / $14.95
VOL. 2 – ACOUSTIC	00699569 / $16.95	**VOL. 46 – MAINSTREAM ROCK**	00699722 / $16.95
VOL. 3 – HARD ROCK	00699573 / $16.95	**VOL. 47 – HENDRIX SMASH HITS**	00699723 / $17.95
VOL. 4 – POP/ROCK	00699571 / $16.99	**VOL. 48 – AEROSMITH CLASSICS**	00699724 / $14.95
VOL. 5 – MODERN ROCK	00699574 / $16.99	**VOL. 49 – STEVIE RAY VAUGHAN**	00699725 / $16.95
VOL. 6 – '90s ROCK	00699572 / $16.99	**VOL. 50 – NÜ METAL**	00699726 / $14.95
VOL. 7 – BLUES	00699575 / $16.95	**VOL. 51 – ALTERNATIVE '90s**	00699727 / $12.95
VOL. 8 – ROCK	00699585 / $14.95	**VOL. 52 – FUNK**	00699728 / $14.95
VOL. 9 – PUNK ROCK	00699576 / $14.95	**VOL. 54 – HEAVY METAL**	00699730 / $14.95
VOL. 10 – ACOUSTIC	00699586 / $16.95	**VOL. 55 – POP METAL**	00699731 / $14.95
VOL. 11 – EARLY ROCK	00699579 / $14.95	**VOL. 56 – FOO FIGHTERS**	00699749 / $14.95
VOL. 12 – POP/ROCK	00699587 / $14.95	**VOL. 57 – SYSTEM OF A DOWN**	00699751 / $14.95
VOL. 13 – FOLK ROCK	00699581 / $14.95	**VOL. 58 – BLINK-182**	00699772 / $14.95
VOL. 14 – BLUES ROCK	00699582 / $16.95	**VOL. 59 – GODSMACK**	00699773 / $14.95
VOL. 15 – R&B	00699583 / $14.95	**VOL. 60 – 3 DOORS DOWN**	00699774 / $14.95
VOL. 16 – JAZZ	00699584 / $15.95	**VOL. 61 – SLIPKNOT**	00699775 / $14.95
VOL. 17 – COUNTRY	00699588 / $15.95	**VOL. 62 – CHRISTMAS CAROLS**	00699798 / $12.95
VOL. 18 – ACOUSTIC ROCK	00699577 / $15.95	**VOL. 63 – CREEDENCE CLEARWATER REVIVAL**	00699802 / $16.99
VOL. 19 – SOUL	00699578 / $14.95	**VOL. 64 – THE ULTIMATE OZZY OSBOURNE**	00699803 / $16.99
VOL. 20 – ROCKABILLY	00699580 / $14.95	**VOL. 65 – THE DOORS**	00699806 / $16.99
VOL. 21 – YULETIDE	00699602 / $14.95	**VOL. 66 – THE ROLLING STONES**	00699807 / $16.95
VOL. 22 – CHRISTMAS	00699600 / $15.95	**VOL. 67 – BLACK SABBATH**	00699808 / $16.99
VOL. 23 – SURF	00699635 / $14.95	**VOL. 68 – PINK FLOYD – DARK SIDE OF THE MOON**	00699809 / $16.99
VOL. 24 – ERIC CLAPTON	00699649 / $16.95	**VOL. 69 – ACOUSTIC FAVORITES**	00699810 / $14.95
VOL. 25 – LENNON & McCARTNEY	00699642 / $14.95	**VOL. 71 – CHRISTIAN ROCK**	00699824 / $14.95
VOL. 26 – ELVIS PRESLEY	00699643 / $14.95	**VOL. 72 – ACOUSTIC '90S**	00699827 / $14.95
VOL. 27 – DAVID LEE ROTH	00699645 / $16.95	**VOL. 74 – PAUL BALOCHE**	00699831 / $14.95
VOL. 28 – GREG KOCH	00699646 / $14.95	**VOL. 75 – TOM PETTY**	00699882 / $16.99
VOL. 29 – BOB SEGER	00699647 / $14.95	**VOL. 76 – COUNTRY HITS**	00699884 / $14.95
VOL. 30 – KISS	00699644 / $14.95	**VOL. 78 – NIRVANA**	00700132 / $14.95
VOL. 31 – CHRISTMAS HITS	00699652 / $14.95	**VOL. 80 – ACOUSTIC ANTHOLOGY**	00700175 / $19.95
VOL. 32 – THE OFFSPRING	00699653 / $14.95	**VOL. 81 – ROCK ANTHOLOGY**	00700176 / $19.95
VOL. 33 – ACOUSTIC CLASSICS	00699656 / $16.95	**VOL. 82 – EASY SONGS**	00700177 / $12.95
VOL. 34 – CLASSIC ROCK	00699658 / $16.95	**VOL. 83 – THREE CHORD SONGS**	00700178 / $12.95
VOL. 35 – HAIR METAL	00699660 / $16.95	**VOL. 96 – THIRD DAY**	00700560 / $14.95
VOL. 36 – SOUTHERN ROCK	00699661 / $16.95	**VOL. 97 – ROCK BAND**	00700703 / $14.95
VOL. 37 – ACOUSTIC METAL	00699662 / $16.95	**VOL. 98 – ROCK BAND**	00700704 / $14.95
VOL. 38 – BLUES	00699663 / $16.95		
VOL. 39 – '80s METAL	00699664 / $16.95		
VOL. 40 – INCUBUS	00699668 / $16.95		
VOL. 41 – ERIC CLAPTON	00699669 / $16.95		
VOL. 42 – CHART HITS	00699670 / $16.95		
VOL. 43 – LYNYRD SKYNYRD	00699681 / $17.95		
VOL. 44 – JAZZ	00699689 / $14.95		

Prices, contents, and availability subject to change without notice.

FOR MORE INFORMATION, SEE YOUR LOCAL MUSIC DEALER,
OR WRITE TO:

HAL•LEONARD® CORPORATION

7777 W. BLUEMOUND RD. P.O. BOX 13819 MILWAUKEE, WI 53213

Visit Hal Leonard online at www.halleonard.com

Complete song lists available online.

GUITAR BIBLES
from **HAL·LEONARD®**

Hal Leonard proudly presents the Guitar Bible series. Each volume contains great songs in authentic, note-for-note transcriptions with lyrics and tablature.

ACOUSTIC GUITAR BIBLE
35 acoustic classics: Angie • Building a Mystery • Change the World • Dust in the Wind • Hold My Hand • Iris • Maggie May • Southern Cross • Tears in Heaven • Wild World • and more.
00690432...$19.95

ACOUSTIC ROCK GUITAR BIBLE
35 classics: And I Love Her • Behind Blue Eyes • Come to My Window • Free Fallin' • Give a Little Bit • More Than Words • Night Moves • Pink Houses • Slide • 3 AM • and more.
00690625...$19.95

BABY BOOMER'S GUITAR BIBLE
35 songs: Angie • Can't Buy Me Love • Happy Together • Hey Jude • Imagine • Laughing • Longer • My Girl • New Kid in Town • Rebel, Rebel • Wild Thing • and more.
00690412...$19.95

BLUES GUITAR BIBLE
35 blues tunes: Boom Boom • Hide Away • I Can't Quit You Baby • I'm Your Hoochie Coochie Man • Killing Floor • Pride and Joy • Sweet Little Angel • The Thrill Is Gone • and more.
00690437...$19.95

BLUES-ROCK GUITAR BIBLE
35 songs: Cross Road Blues (Crossroads) • Hide Away • The House Is Rockin' • Love Struck Baby • Move It On Over • Piece of My Heart • Statesboro Blues • You Shook Me • more.
00690450...$19.95

CLASSIC ROCK GUITAR BIBLE
33 essential rock songs: Beast of Burden • Cat Scratch Fever • Double Vision • Free Ride • Hard to Handle • Life in the Fast Lane • The Stroke • Won't Get Fooled Again • and more.
00690662...$19.95

COUNTRY GUITAR BIBLE
35 country classics: Ain't Goin' Down • Blue Eyes Crying in the Rain • Boot Scootin' Boogie • Friends in Low Places • I'm So Lonesome I Could Cry • T-R-O-U-B-L-E • and more.
00690465...$19.95

DISCO GUITAR BIBLE
30 stand-out songs from the disco days: Brick House • Disco Inferno • Funkytown • Get Down Tonight • I Love the Night Life • Le Freak • Stayin' Alive • Y.M.C.A. • and more.
00690627...$17.95

EARLY ROCK GUITAR BIBLE
35 fantastic classics: Blue Suede Shoes • Do Wah Diddy Diddy • Hang On Sloopy • I'm a Believer • Louie, Louie • Oh, Pretty Woman • Surfin' U.S.A. • Twist and Shout • and more.
00690680...$17.95

FOLK-ROCK GUITAR BIBLE
35 songs: At Seventeen • Blackbird • Fire and Rain • Happy Together • Leaving on a Jet Plane • Our House • Time in a Bottle • Turn! Turn! Turn! • You've Got a Friend • more.
00690464...$19.95

GRUNGE GUITAR BIBLE
30 songs: All Apologies • Counting Blue Cars • Glycerine • Jesus Christ Pose • Lithium • Man in the Box • Nearly Lost You • Smells like Teen Spirit • This Is a Call • Violet • and more.
00690649...$17.95

HARD ROCK GUITAR BIBLE
35 songs: Ballroom Blitz • Bang a Gong • Barracuda • Living After Midnight • Rock You like a Hurricane • School's Out • Welcome to the Jungle • You Give Love a Bad Name • more.
00690453...$19.95

INSTRUMENTAL GUITAR BIBLE
37 great instrumentals: Always with Me, Always with You • Green Onions • Hide Away • Jessica • Linus and Lucy • Perfidia • Satch Boogie • Tequila • Walk Don't Run • and more.
00690514...$19.95

JAZZ GUITAR BIBLE
31 songs: Body and Soul • In a Sentimental Mood • My Funny Valentine • Nuages • Satin Doll • So What • Star Dust • Take Five • Tangerine • Yardbird Suite • and more.
00690466...$19.95

MODERN ROCK GUITAR BIBLE
26 rock favorites: Aerials (System of a Down) • Alive (P.O.D.) • Cold Hard Bitch (Jet) • Kryptonite (3 Doors Down) • Like a Stone (Audioslave) • Whatever (Godsmack) • and more.
00690724...$19.95

NÜ METAL GUITAR BIBLE
25 edgy metal hits: Aenema • Black • Edgecrusher • Last Resort • People of the Sun • Schism • Southtown • Take a Look Around • Toxicity • Youth of the Nation • and more.
00690569...$19.95

POP/ROCK GUITAR BIBLE
35 pop hits: Change the World • Heartache Tonight • Money for Nothing • Mony, Mony • Pink Houses • Smooth • Summer of '69 • 3 AM • What I Like About You • and more.
00690517...$19.95

R&B GUITAR BIBLE
35 R&B classics: Brick House • Fire • I Got You (I Feel Good) • Love Rollercoaster • Shining Star • Sir Duke • Super Freak • and more.
00690452...$19.95

ROCK GUITAR BIBLE
33 songs: All Day and All of the Night • Born to Be Wild • Day Tripper • Hey Joe • Jailhouse Rock • Money • Paranoid • Sultans of Swing • Walk This Way • You Really Got Me • more!
00690313...$19.95

ROCKABILLY GUITAR BIBLE
31 songs from artists such as Elvis, Buddy Holly and the Brian Setzer Orchestra: Blue Suede Shoes • Hello Mary Lou • Peggy Sue • Rock This Town • Travelin' Man • and more.
00690570...$19.95

SOUL GUITAR BIBLE
33 songs: Groovin' • I've Been Loving You Too Long • Let's Get It On • My Girl • Respect • Theme from Shaft • Soul Man • and more.
00690506...$19.95

SOUTHERN ROCK GUITAR BIBLE
25 southern rock classics: Can't You See • Free Bird • Hold On Loosely • La Grange • Midnight Rider • Sweet Home Alabama • and more.
00690723...$19.95

Prices, contents, and availability subject to change without notice.

FOR MORE INFORMATION, SEE YOUR LOCAL MUSIC DEALER, OR WRITE TO:

HAL·LEONARD®
CORPORATION
7777 W. BLUEMOUND RD. P.O. BOX 13819 MILWAUKEE, WI 53213

Visit Hal Leonard online at **www.halleonard.com**

0606